Pope John Paul II

Pope John Paul II boards plane in Ottawa to head back to Rome after his 12-day tour of Canada in 1984. (Paul Chiasson/CP)

Pope John Paul II waves to faithful at his summer residence near Rome in 1997. (Plinio Lepri/AP)

Pope John Paul II
CONNECTING TO CANADIANS

Foreword by Dr. Michael Higgins

Edited by Patti Tasko
with files from The Canadian Press

Photo Editor: Ron Poling

John Wiley & Sons Canada Ltd.

Library and Archives Canada Cataloguing in Publication

Pope John Paul II : connecting to Canadians.

ISBN-13 978-0-470-83516-8
ISBN-10 0-470-83516-8

1. John Paul II, Pope, 1920-2005. 2. John Paul II, Pope, 1920-2005 —Travel—Canada.
BX1378.5.P65 2005   282'.092   C2005-901456-3

Production Credits:

Text editor: Patti Tasko, The Canadian Press
Photo editors: Ron Poling, Graeme Roy, The Canadian Press
Cover design: Ian Koo
Interior design: Adrian So R.G.D.
Front cover photo: Jose More, The Canadian Press
Back cover photo: Vatican Pool, The Canadian Press
Printer: Transcontinental

John Wiley & Sons Canada, Ltd.
6045 Freemont Blvd.,
Mississauga, Ontario
L5R 4J3

Printed in Canada
10 9 8 7 6 5 4 3 2 1

Dear Reader,

This publication is a collection of our most prized images. Some of the images you may have seen before in your local newspaper. Others you may be seeing for the first time.

High-quality prints of many of the photographs in this book may be purchased for personal use.

For information about acquiring CP images, please visit us at http://www.cp.org/prints or contact CP at 1-800-434-7578 or archives@cpimages.ca

Page 1

Page 24

Page 74

Page 85

Contents

Foreword

By Dr. Michael Higgins,
President, St. Jerome's University

Pope John Paul II was not averse to travelling. The role of a pilgrim is to travel, after all, and one of the more onerous and yet joy-filled duties of the Supreme Pontiff of the Roman Catholic Church is to "connect" with his flock, a flock that is by its nature widespread and diverse.

From the inception of his pontificate in 1978, John Paul made clear to the world his determination to bring the liberating message of the gospel to all who hunger to hear it. He was quite prepared to bring it to those disinclined to hear it as well. And he did this— the countless days of travel, the sermons, speeches, media events, rallies, private sessions, grand liturgies, epic walkabouts, and incalculable hours of sleep deprivation—precisely because he understood that his job description meant that he was obligated to "connect" with other pilgrims on the planet.

◀ A Swiss guard stands at attention before the Pope's weekly general audience in the Paul VI Hall at the Vatican in 2003. (Plinio Lepri/AP)

▲ The Pope in Vancouver in 1984. (Vatican Pool/CP)

And John Paul was a pilgrim, one who undertook to go on a peregrinatio, a peregrination, a "going forth into strange countries." He did this regularly during his long papacy—this going forth into foreign lands—because peregrinations are not only a wonderful opportunity for effective evangelizing, for bringing the mission of the church to untold millions, but also for discovering something about oneself, the pilgrim. John Paul's principal tool for educating himself in his job as the Successor of St. Peter, Primate of Italy, Servant of the servants of God, Patriarch of the West, Head of the Vatican City State, and Bishop of Rome was to get out and see, taste, and hear the joys and anxieties of his time. In order to do that, the Chief Shepherd traversed the globe.

He came to Canada three times—1984, 1987, and 2002—and he used every opportunity, even when limited by his deteriorating health, to meet with the

young and the indigenous peoples. He spoke eloquently and forcefully about the moral and dogmatic truths of the Roman Catholic Church, reiterated the constant teaching of the tradition, celebrated human rights and dignity, proclaimed the joy inherent in authentic Christian living, and critiqued contemporary culture wherever he found it wanting.

As importantly, the Pope could see with his own eyes the impressive multiculturalism that goes so far in defining the Canadian reality. John Paul could also see the natural wealth, economic prosperity, political freedom, intellectual vibrancy, and sheer youthfulness of Canada, such a new land to his often tired and occasionally sad European eyes.

◀ John Paul II and Mother Teresa at St. Peter's Basilica in 1997. (Arturo Mari/AP)

▲ Pope John Paul II at the Death Wall memorial to Holocaust victims in Auschwitz, Poland in 1979. (AP)

John Paul knew that the pilgrim learns as much as he shares, that a true peregrination is an act of reciprocity, and he knew that a true leader must listen as much as he speaks, that a true leader is more pastoral than oracular, more the brother than the overlord.

The photographs and words herein tell a moving story about this papal conversation with Canada: the open embrace, the welcoming smile, the wide benediction, the gentle touch, the recollected pose, the affectionate kiss. Karol Wojtyla of Krakow, John Paul II of Rome, world pilgrim for so many years, understood tactility, relished the photo op, knew intimately the human craving for drama and communion, and possessed an insatiable interest in all cultures and languages.

This very same pilgrim came to Canada to teach and to learn. In other words: to connect.

◀ Pope Paul VI, left, greets his eventual successor, Archbishop Karol Wojtyla of Krakow, at the Vatican in an undated photo. (AP)

Michael W. Higgins is author of the award-winning *Heretic Blood: The Spiritual Geography of Thomas Merton*, co-author of the national bestseller *Power and Peril: The Catholic Church at the Crossroads*, and President of St. Jerome's University in Waterloo, Ontario.

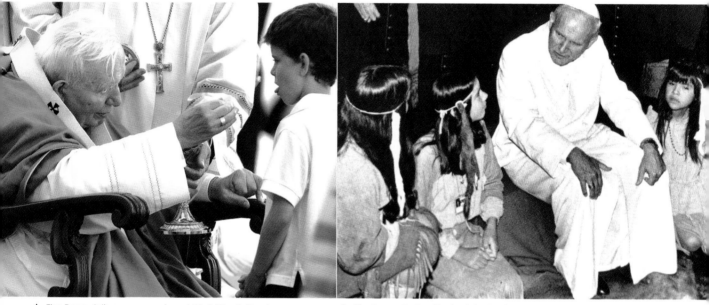

▲ The Pope delivers communion at World Youth Day in Toronto in 2002. (Gabriel Bouys/Pool/CP)

▲ The Pope chats with aboriginal children at Ste-Marie-Among-the-Hurons in 1984. (Ryan Remiorz/UPC/CP)

Introduction

By James McCarten and Patti Tasko

▲ Josef Cardinal Glemp, primate of Poland, blesses a bronze sculpture of Pope John Paul in Brampton, Ont., in 2002. (Kevin Frayer/CP)

It was a massive spectacle of faith unmatched in Canadian history, with a stooped, tremulous shadow of a man at its centre, a rickety raft of old age buoyed by oceans of youthful Catholic enthusiasm. But there was no mistaking the power of Pope John Paul II during those seven days in Toronto in July 2002.

"You are young, and the Pope is old . . . but he still identifies with your hopes and aspirations," John Paul told more than 500,000 rapt Catholics attending World Youth Day events, during what would be his last visit to Canada. Every low, muffled word was a visible struggle, every trembling wave a painful reminder of his failing health. But the young people gathered to see the Pope were as much an inspiration for him as he was to them.

"I have seen enough evidence to be unshakably convinced that no difficulty, no fear is so great that it can completely suffocate the hope that springs eternal in the hearts of the young," he said. "Do not let that hope die. Stake your lives on it."

It was in his relentless travels that John Paul, the most travelled pope in history and one often described as a travelling salesman for the Roman Catholic Church, defined his tenure as Holy Father. His three papal trips to Canada—a 12-day, cross-country odyssey in 1984, followed by briefer visits in 1987 and 2002—helped fortify an already strong bond with Canada's Catholic community.

John Paul had visited Canada before he was named Pope. In 1969, as Karol Cardinal Wojtyla, he visited Polish communities in Toronto, Montreal, Edmonton, Calgary and other cities at the invitation of the Canadian Polish Congress. He also made a side trip to southern Ontario in 1976 after leading a delegation of Polish bishops to the International Eucharistic Congress in Philadelphia.

> "I am increasingly aware that the day is drawing near when I will have to present myself to God and make an accounting of my whole life."
> *–Pope John Paul II, May 2003, at the Vatican*

The 1984 trip was a pastoral pilgrimage that took him from the outports of Newfoundland to B.C. Place in Vancouver. He visited the touchstones of Roman Catholicism

▲ The Pope during a vacation in the Italian Alps in 2000. (Arturo Mari/AP)

in Canada, including the shrine of Ste-Anne-de-Beaupré and St. Joseph's Oratory in Quebec and the Martyrs' Shrine in Midland, Ontario. He preached in person to hundreds of thousands in outdoor masses and reached millions more in extended television coverage, speaking of faith and hope, justice and peace. The silver-haired pontiff, his stooped posture the legacy of a would-be assassin's bullet in

> "We grew up like other boys in our hometown, doing things that most boys do. But with Karol there was no time for the usual childhood mischief or pranks – he never went for that sort of thing, although he had fun, too, and was a friendly and likable lad."
>
> *-Rudolf Kogler of Toronto, childhood friend of Pope John Paul II, in 1984*

1981, blessed Newfoundland fishermen in their boats and tapped his toe at a concert with young people. In Ottawa, organizers sent him cruising down the Rideau Canal in a bubble-topped boat. The parade routes and various papal venues were festooned with white and gold banners and flags bearing the tiara and crossed keys, the symbols of the papacy. One Montreal site alone was decorated with 10,000 plants and flowers.

The only major glitch was the cancellation, because of fog, of a visit to Fort Simpson in the Northwest Territories. That was remedied in September 1987 when the Pope added a five-hour visit onto an exhausting American tour. Standing beneath a towering, stylized teepee, the Pope told an audience of about 5,000 mostly Dene people – many of whom had travelled for days across the North to get there – that they were entitled to self-government.

By his final visit to Canada, for World Youth Day in 2002, the once-robust pontiff was a fragile old man, visibly suffering the symptoms of Parkinson's disease. But that summer, awaited by more than half a million Christian youth who came to Toronto for the gathering, Pope John Paul spent seven days flouting the indignities of infirmity, tackling airplane staircases without trepidation and immersing himself in his papal duties with visible delight.

◀ Karol Wojtyla, 19, in July 1939 in what was then eastern Poland. (Adam Gatty-Kostyal/AP)

During a boat cruise he welcomed residents from a nearby home for the developmentally disabled to an impromptu blessing atop the waves of central Ontario's Lake Simcoe. He even ventured outside the security of his bulletproof popemobile to greet Toronto residents before meeting hundreds of thousands of young disciples for a Saturday night vigil and three-hour Sunday mass. "The world you are inheriting is a world which desperately needs a new sense of brotherhood and human solidarity," he told more than 800,000 people from a colossal stage adorned with a 50-metre cross. "It is a world which needs to be touched and healed by the beauty and richness of God's love. It needs witnesses to that love. It needs you to be the salt of the earth and the light of the world."

◀ Cubans ride by billboard welcoming Pope John Paul before his visit to the island in 1998. (Jose Goitia/CP)

The Pope leaves via helicopter after the papal mass at World Youth Day in ▶ Toronto in 2002. (Aaron Harris/CP)

"It just shows that no matter how old you get, how worn out your body gets, your spirit is pure and your spirit will live forever," said a weeping 17-year-old Donna Lajeunesse-Young, from Bowmanville, Ontario, as the Pope's plane taxied away. "In faith and in God, you can do anything; as long as your heart's in it, you've got the power."

Under different circumstances, the man who became Pope John Paul II might have been a professional athlete, a poet, a playwright or an actor. As a younger man in his native Poland, Karol Josef Wojtyla was involved in all these pursuits. He played soccer, skied, went camping and later had several of his poems and a play published. But at university, his long-held interests in philosophy and religion became focused and he determined to devote his life to the church.

Karol, born May 18, 1920, in Wadowice, Poland, and his brother Edmund, who died of scarlet fever in 1932, grew up in an atmosphere of strict discipline and religious piety. The Pope's official biographer has noted that their father, a lieutenant in the Polish army, made them study in cold rooms to harden them against the elements and to instill spiritual rigour.

One of the participants in the Toronto mass ▶ holds up a cross. (Tom Hanson/CP)

In 1938, Wojtyla went to Jagiellonian University in Warsaw to study dramatic language and literature. There he came under the influence of the Christian mystic Jan Tyranowski, who cultivated his religious and philosophical interests.

Then the Second World War began and Wojtyla started his seminary studies in secret. To avoid deportation or imprisonment by the Nazi occupiers of Poland, he worked as a manual labourer in a quarry and at a chemical factory. Meanwhile, he was involved in a Christian underground movement that fought attempts by the Nazis to suppress Polish culture. In 1944, he went into hiding in the palace of Archbishop Adam Steven Saphieba when his name was reported to be on a Nazi blacklist.

The war ended and a Soviet-backed Communist government was elected in Poland. Wojtyla completed his studies and in 1946 was ordained. He was sent to France, where he did pastoral work among Polish refugees and French working-class youth.

He went to Rome's Pontifical Angelicum University to study philosophy under the eminent French Dominican Reginald Garrigou-Lagrange, described as an uncompromising traditionalist who contributed to the future pope's conservatism. Wojtyla got a doctorate in philosophy and another PhD in theology before he returned to Krakow. He taught in the theology department of Jagiellonian University until it was closed by the Communist government, then at the Catholic University in Lublin. During this teaching period, he wrote a number of moral and philosophical works as well as poems and the play.

He was camping with students in 1958 when he learned he had been named auxiliary bishop of Krakow. He was appointed archbishop in 1964 and named a cardinal three years later.

He attended the historic Second Vatican Council between 1962 and 1965. Speaking on behalf of Polish bishops, he joined others from eastern Europe in insisting on a strong statement on religious freedom in Communist countries.

▲ Pope John Paul visits the Western Wall in Jerusalem in 2000. (Jerome Delay/AP)

▲ The Pope with Marc Cardinal Ouellet, Archbishop of Quebec, at a 2003 ceremony at the Vatican where John Paul promoted Ouellet and 29 other men to the title of cardinal. (Massimo Sambucetti/AP)

In staunchly Catholic Poland, Karol Cardinal Wojtyla earned a reputation as a shrewd statesman who understood the importance of pushing a Polish national identity. He was instrumental in formulating the Polish church's moderate but firm demands for religious freedom in a Communist state.

His predecessor, Pope John Paul I, had been in the church's top job for only 33 days when he died unexpectedly in September 1978. The church's cardinals found themselves once again gathering at the Sistine Chapel to select a new pope. It took two days of voting by the 111 cardinal-electors to elect Karol Cardinal Wojtyla on October 16, 1978. The indecision of the early balloting was marked in the traditional way, by burning the ballots and sending plumes of black smoke up the chapel's smokestack – to ensure the message was clear, Vatican officials also burned black army flares for a minute before igniting the ballots. The traditional white smoke announcing a new pope, helped by a white army flare, billowed into the night at 6:18 p.m.

Taking the name John Paul II, Wojtyla was the first non-Italian to be chosen in over 400 years, and at 58 he was the youngest pope in over 130 years. Despite describing himself as "full of trepidation," he quickly projected a decisive style, whether meeting at the Vatican with his bishops at working lunches—something unheard of under previous pontiffs—or speaking out on human rights at packed public audiences.

Fluent in half a dozen languages including English, John Paul took his message to the world. His tours

▲ Pope John Paul and Mother Teresa ride in the popemobile outside the Home of the Dying in Calcutta, India in 1986. (AP)

▲ Pope John Paul II speaks with Mehmet Ali Agca, who shot him in a 1981 assassination attempt, in Agca's prison cell in Rome, in this undated photo. (Arturo Mari/AP)

abroad attracted millions—both Catholics and non-Catholics—into the streets and to outdoor masses to see and hear him.

His early dramatic training was exhibited in his mastery of crowds. His warm, vivid personality charmed everyone from children to Marxist presidents in Africa. But, in the early years of his papacy, it was his stamina that was most impressive. He was perhaps the most athletic of the modern popes—he skied when he had the opportunity. During his first visit as Pope to Canada, his activities lasted 12 hours or more each of the 12 days, with only one real break.

The first attack on his physical vigour came in 1981, when a Turkish gunman shot him in the abdomen in an assassination attempt in St. Peter's Square. Although it

took him a year to recover from the wound, the powerfully built John Paul resumed his strenuous world travels. There was another attempt on the Pope's life at Fatima, Portugal, in 1982 when a man lunged at him with a knife.

From the mid-1990s on, John Paul suffered from Parkinson's disease and crippling knee and hip ailments. He continued his work and travels – the Vatican devised a throne-like chair on wheels that allowed him to celebrate mass while seated. Chairlifts helped him to and from planes. Speech became a problem; often others read his words in public. By the 25th anniversary of his papacy, he was the picture of extreme fragility yet sheer determination, of surprising resilience under severe physical limitations.

Although he continued to appear in public, and the Vatican regularly reported that he was continuing to fulfill his papal duties, by early 2005 the Pope's health was clearly severely limiting his ability to function. In February he was rushed twice to the hospital with flu-like systems. He had surgery to insert a breathing tube, which affected his ability to speak, and then had a feeding tube inserted to rebuild his strength. John Paul managed to say a few words to the public on March 13. It turned out to be the last time.

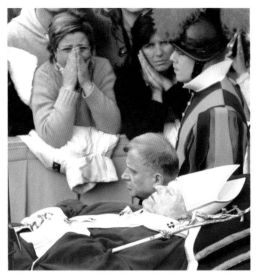

On March 27, for the first time since his papacy began in 1978, Easter Sunday mass at the Vatican was celebrated without him. He appeared at his window overlooking St. Peter's Square for several moments, but managed only a few sounds before he gave up and delivered his Easter blessing with a sign of the cross. A similar scene was repeated three days later when John Paul tried to utter a few words after an aide read greetings and prayers. Like Easter Sunday, many in the crowd had tears in their eyes as they saw the Pope's futile efforts to speak.

On April 1 spokesman Joaquin Navarro-Valls choked up as he told reporters about the 84-year-old pope's worsening condition. In St. Peter's Square thousands of pilgrims gathered to pray for him. Around the world, millions more did the same.

By the evening of April 2, the crowd at the Vatican had reached tens of thousands when the news of his death came. In contrast to the church's ancient traditions, Navarro-Valls announced it in an e-mail to journalists. He said officials were following instructions that John Paul had written for them in 1996.

Those gathered outside the Pope's apartments fell silent at the news. Then they started to clap – an Italian tradition to show appreciation for important figures who have passed away. Many wept as others tried to comfort them.

In Canada and around the world, church bells rang out to mark the death. People of all religions expressed their admiration for John Paul. "This man changed the face of the papacy, he was always on the way, always on to the next mission," said Marc Cardinal Ouellet, Archbishop of Quebec, as tears ran down his cheeks. "We all feel like orphans at this moment."

Above left: Pope John Paul II's body is carried to St. Peter's Basilica. (Andrew Medichini/AP)
Above right: Mourners leave flowers at a statue of the Pope in Toronto. (Frank Gunn/CP)
Below right: A mother and her son attend a memorial service at Holy Rosary Cathedral in Vancouver. (Richard Lam/CP)
Below left: Tens of thousands crowd St. Peter's Square to attend a mass for the repose of the Pope's soul. (Andrew Medichinii/AP)

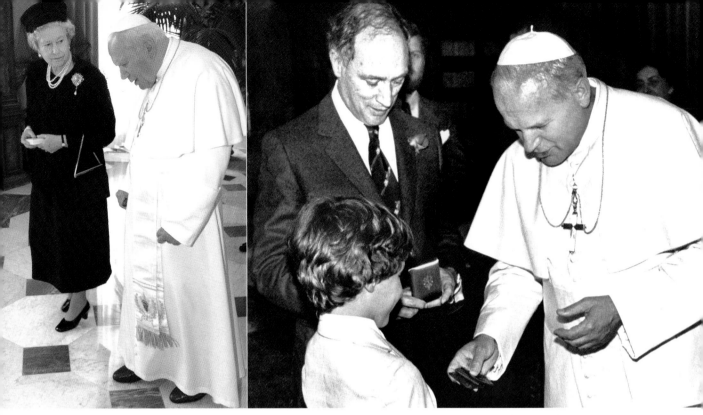

▲ The Pope and Queen Elizabeth at the Vatican in 2000. (Alessandro Bianchi/ Pool/AP)

▲ Prime Minister Pierre Trudeau and his son Justin meet the Pope in Rome in 1980. (Fred Chartrand/CP)

John Paul was the third-longest serving pontiff. Christ's chosen apostle, Peter, considered the first pope, holds the top position. At 26 years, five months and 17 days, John Paul was second to only one other "regular" pope, Pius IX, a 19th-century pontiff who held the job for 32 years. That has certainly earned him a special place among the 263 successors of Peter in the past 2,000 years.

Statistics aside, John Paul II is also, unquestionably, among the most important religious figures of the last century. This is a pope who will be remembered for helping to end Communist rule in eastern Europe by sparking what amounted to a peaceful revolution in his homeland; for seeking to heal divisions between Christians and Jews; and for travelling around the globe to greet his one-billion-member flock.

▲ Cuban President Fidel Castro arrives at the Vatican to meet the Pope in 1996. (Arturo Mari/AP)

▲ The Pope and U.S. President Ronald Reagan in Miami in 1987. (Scott Stewart/AP)

He was a constant voice for peace. In 1984 he stepped in and mediated a territorial dispute between Chile and Argentina when the two mainly Catholic South American neighbours were on the brink of war. John Paul was more successful there than in opposing both the 1991 Gulf War and the U.S.-led invasion of Iraq in 2003. That didn't stop him from repeatedly denouncing violence committed in the name of religion, especially after the September 11, 2001, attacks. His efforts to draw the attention of the world's richest countries to the developing world's debt burden drew almost 700,000 Canadians to sign a petition in 1999 urging government debt relief.

He also tried to develop warmer relations between Catholics and Jews. He extended the Vatican's full diplomatic recognition to Israel and was the first pontiff to visit the main synagogue in Rome. He regularly attacked anti-Semitism and issued a statement of Christian contrition over the Holocaust. He visited the Middle East several times, including a six-day pilgrimage to Jerusalem in 2000 that included a trip to the Western Wall, Judaism's holiest shrine.

He also took Canadians to task on certain issues. During a November 1990 meeting at the Vatican, the pontiff quizzed then-prime minister Brian Mulroney about the breakdown of a land claims settlement with the Dene Nation, the same group he had travelled so

◀ John Paul in the Italian Alps in 1998. (Arturo Mari/Vatican Pool/AP)

▲ Karol Wojtyla (right) at a military camp in July 1939 in what was then eastern Poland. (Adam Gatty-Kostyal/AP)

far to meet three years earlier. Not that the Roman Catholic Church's record on aboriginal issues was spotless. During John Paul's reign, the church came under fire repeatedly for its role in running residential schools for Canadian aboriginal children. And during his watch Roman Catholic institutions in Canada were also at the centre of major sex scandals, most notably the now-closed Mount Cashel orphanage for boys in St. John's, Newfoundland. In 1993, John Paul told bishops from Atlantic Canada during a visit to Rome that sexual scandal "has been a source of great suffering for the church in Canada."

He had his critics. Many were angered by his unbending, conservative stance on social issues. He supported church law barring women from the priesthood and priests from marrying and he maintained a firm opposition to birth control and abortion. Some blamed his stance against birth control for worsening the AIDS crisis in Africa. He endorsed a worldwide campaign to keep same-sex unions from receiving legal recognition. Late in his pontificate he wrote an encyclical – a special letter reserved for matters of extreme importance to the church – reminding divorced Catholics who remarry not to take communion. Roman Catholics were also warned against taking communion in non-Catholic churches.

Apart from this criticism, his papacy had its setbacks. John Paul often lamented that the countries of

eastern Europe escaped the totalitarianism of Soviet Communism only to be corrupted by western consumerism. Another major sorrow came from his inability to achieve reconciliation with the Orthodox Church. Beyond theological differences over papal supremacy, relations with the Russian Orthodox Church worsened after the fall of Communism. Alarmed that the Vatican was trying to make missionary advances into traditional Orthodox territory, leaders thwarted John Paul's desire to become the first pope to visit Russia.

More revelations of priestly sex abuse, mainly in Europe and the United States, and attempts by bishops to cover molestation charges rocked the church late in John Paul's pontificate. He spoke out several times, telling young Catholics attending World Youth Day in Toronto in 2002 that the "harm done by some priests and religious to the young and vulnerable fills us all with a deep sense of sadness and shame." The Vatican did sign off on a toughened policy for dealing with clerical molesters in the United States, but critics said it was slow to acknowledge the problem.

John Paul's supporters will argue that his accomplishments far outweigh the problems of his pontificate.

For the millions of people who attended mass with him and admired his tenacity and holiness, his legacy may well be a more personal one.

Take the case of André Chiasson, a Moncton electrician. The Vatican credits a Quebec nun, Dina Belanger, with saving his life as a baby in 1939, a decade after her death. To the amazement of doctors, Chiasson recovered completely from hydrocephalus, an often-fatal brain disease, after his mother held a prayer vigil to Belanger. Chiasson grew up feeling ambivalent about the attention he'd received because of his miraculous recovery and had to be persuaded to join a Canadian delegation that went to the Vatican in 1993 when the Pope added Belanger to the ranks of blessed souls, the last step before sainthood. After the two-hour ceremony, Chiasson and his wife had a brief audience with the Pope.

"He blessed our family," said Chiasson. "It was quite an experience. I can't find words to describe what I saw."

– With files from Larry Black and Michelle MacAfee, The Canadian Press; Victor Simpson, the Associated Press.

◀ Pope John Paul and former concentration camp prisoners at Auschwitz, Poland in 1979. (AP)

A look at the life of Pope John Paul II

May 18, 1920:
Born Karol Joseph Wojtyla in
Wadowice, Poland.

June 20, 1920:
Baptized by P. Franciszek Zak, a military chaplain.

September 15, 1926:
Enters elementary school for boys.

April 13, 1929:
His mother dies.

June 1930:
Admitted to Marcin Wadowita, state secondary
school for boys.

December 5, 1932:
His brother Edmund dies.

1934-1938:
Performs in student theatre in Wadowice.

May 1938:
Receives the sacrament of confirmation.

June 22, 1938:
Enrols in the philosophy faculty at Jagiellonian
University, Krakow.

July 1939:
Attends university military training for Polish and
Ukrainian students.

November 1, 1940:
Earns a living as a stone cutter in a quarry near Krakow,
forestalling deportation and imprisonment.

October 1942:
Begins clandestine studies for the priesthood in
Krakow's underground seminary; registers in the
theology faculty at Jagiellonian University.

August 1943:
Archbishop Adam Stefan Sapieha transfers him and
other clandestine seminarians to the archbishop's
residence. He remains there until the end of the war.

November 1, 1946:
Ordained a priest.

November 2, 1946:
Celebrates his first mass in the crypt of St. Leonard at
Wavel, Poland.

November 15, 1946:
Leaves Poland to begin studies in Rome.

July 8, 1948:
Sent as assistant pastor to Niegowic
near Gdow, Poland.

August 1949:
Recalled to Krakow to be assistant pastor at
St. Florian's.

July 4, 1958:
Appointed auxiliary bishop of Krakow.

September 28, 1958:
Ordained bishop in Wavel Cathedral.

October-December 1962:
Participates in the first session of the Second Vatican
Council.

October-December 1963:
Participates in the second session of the Second
Vatican Council.

March 8, 1964:
Installed as metropolitan bishop of Krakow.

September-November 1964:
Participates in the third session of the Second Vatican
Council.

September-December 1965:
Participates in fourth session and closing of the
Second Vatican Council.

June 28, 1967:
Consecrated cardinal in the Sistine Chapel by Pope
Paul VI.

July-August 1969:
Tours Canada.

July 23-September 5, 1976:
Visits the United States and Canada.

August 11-12, 1978:
Attends funeral of Pope Paul VI.

Oct. 3-4, 1978:
Attends funeral of Pope John Paul I.

October 16, 1978:
Elected Pope by cardinals. He is the first Polish pope ever
and the first non-Italian one in 455 years.

January 25, 1979:
First trip abroad as Pope, to Dominican Republic,
Mexico and Bahamas.

June 2, 1979:
First trip back to Poland as Pope.

A portrait of Christ at Exhibition Place in Toronto during World Youth Day 2002. (Kevin Frayer/CP)

September 29, 1979:
Travels to Ireland and United States.

May 13, 1981:
Shot in abdomen by Turkish extremist in St. Peter's Square.

September 9-20, 1984:
First papal visit to Canada.

April 13, 1986:
Makes historic visit to Rome's main synagogue.

September 20, 1987:
Makes a five-hour visit to Fort Simpson, N.W.T., during a U.S. trip to honour a promise he made when his 1984 visit to the hamlet was cancelled by fog.

December 1, 1989:
Meets with Mikhail Gorbachev at the Vatican, first ever meeting between a pope and a Kremlin chief. Establishes diplomatic ties between Vatican and Russia.

May 1, 1991:
Issues first encyclical on social issues since the fall of Communism in Europe, giving qualified approval to capitalism but warning the rich against exploiting the poor.

July 15, 1992:
Operation for benign tumour on colon.

October 31, 1992:
Formally declares the church erred in condemning Galileo.

October 5, 1993:
Issues encyclical *Splendour of Truth*, major statement defending absolute morals against liberal theologians.

November 11, 1993:
Dislocates right shoulder in fall down steps at Vatican event, requiring surgery.

December 30, 1993:
Agreement signed establishing formal ties between Vatican and Israel.

April 29, 1994:
Breaks leg in fall and undergoes hip replacement surgery.

October 19, 1994:
His book, *Beyond the Threshold of Hope*, is published.

October 8, 1996:
Surgery to remove appendix.

March 1, 1999:
Vatican confirms that the Pope has waived the five-year waiting period and begun beatification process for Mother Teresa.

March 20-26, 2000:
Makes first trip as Pope to Holy Land, expresses sorrow for suffering of Jews at Christian hands in note left at Jerusalem's Western Wall.

September 11, 2001:
Condemns "unspeakable horror" of September 11 attacks.

April 23, 2002:
Meets with U.S. cardinals to discuss sex abuse scandal; says there is no place in priesthood for clerics who abuse the young.

July 23-29, 2002:
Visits Toronto to preside over World Youth Day, a gathering of hundreds of thousands of Catholics from around the world.

February 14, 2003:
Receives Iraqi deputy prime minister Tariq Aziz on eve of war.

June 5-9, 2003:
Makes 100th foreign trip, visiting Croatia.

July 31, 2003:
Vatican launches global campaign against gay marriages.

February 2005:
Hospitalized twice for serious breathing problems; undergoes surgery.

Feb. 22, 2005:
His fifth book, *Memory and Identity*, is officially launched.

March 27, 2005:
Appears in public on Easter. Tries to speak but fails.

April 2, 2005:
Vatican announces "the Holy Father died this evening at 9:37 p.m. in his private apartment."

Pope John Paul kisses the ground after arriving in
Quebec City. (Vatican Pool/CP)

1984
Pope John Paul's first visit to Canada

Quebec City
Day One: September 9, 1984

The red carpet was vacuumed, the runway was scrubbed clean, and then a military truck loaded with explosives was trundled to the end of the airport in Quebec City. A man of peace being greeted with a 21-gun salute?

It was the first of many contradictions that echoed throughout Pope John Paul's tour of Canada in 1984. Even the 64-year-old pontiff looked taken aback by the first thunderous boom in the Sunday morning sunshine in Quebec City. But John Paul quickly recovered his poise, kneeling to kiss a spotless piece of Canadian concrete before he went on to meet the 600 dignitaries waiting to welcome him. "I bring with me the love, the joy, the pain and the hope of your brothers and sisters all over the world," he said, speaking in both French and English.

After a year of planning, the Pope had finally touched Canadian soil to begin what was then his longest-ever visit to one country. His first stop – Quebec, 87 per cent Catholic – provided a particular contradiction. The Pope said he started his trip here because it was the oldest church diocese in North America. It was also home to half of Canada's Catholics. But this seeming fortress of the church was, in fact, crumbling at the foundation, and badly.

A poll released on the eve of the Pope's visit showed an overwhelming rejection by Quebec Catholics of many of the tenets of John Paul's faith. The skyline of this province remained dotted with church spires, but inside many of those commanding white stone bastions the pews were empty. "I thank God that I had the chance to see him before I die," said Jean-Guy Grancher of Val Belair, Quebec, as he watched the pontiff. "But I'd say he's come 25 years too late. Nobody goes to church anymore."

But if Quebec had moved away forever from a state governed by the Catholic Church, Quebecers still seemed unable to turn their backs on one of the most popular popes in history. Many came out to see him, lining the streets and standing in balconies waving papal flags. Some were just curious, but others were left speechless. "I'm totally taken aback," said a bus driver who had just shaken the Pope's hand. "When a saint like that touches you, it's . . ."

It was the peculiar dichotomy that Pope John Paul often provoked among modern-day Catholics: they loved and respected the man, but they couldn't always support where he took the church. Some observers said that his refusal to shy away from controversy was part of the attraction. Unlike western politicians, he didn't govern by polls. "You know you are listening to an honest man," said Msgr. Dennis Murphy, who helped organize the 1984 tour on behalf of the Canadian Conference of Catholic Bishops. "You know he's not there to win a popularity contest."

Throughout his papacy, many Catholics, at least in the West, hoped the Pope would soften the church's stand against artificial birth control. It never happened, but that didn't stop many from using it. At a time when most people condoned premarital sex and accepted homosexuality, he took public stands against both. At a time when priests and members of religious orders were questioning

the theological grounds for celibacy, John Paul urged them to remain "eunuchs for the sake of the kingdom of heaven." At a time when the church had a debilitating shortage of priests, he refused to allow the ordination of women. When asked, during the flight to Canada, to react to criticism of his stance, the Pope said: "I respect everybody. I love everybody. But the truth must always be defended."

Still, Canadians stood on rooftops and in fields in 1984, waiting to glimpse the Pope. Everywhere he went, thousands cheered him on. Masses were attended by hundreds of thousands. In some spots the crowds were smaller than anticipated, but that might have been a result of bad weather, traffic congestion and wall-to-wall live television coverage.

The Pope's first day in Canada was as gruelling as the rest of the tour – from the massive welcome to a popemobile tour through Quebec City, stopping in Cartier-Brébeuf Park to meet 200 newly confirmed young people, then a visit to the Chapel of the Minor Seminary and the tomb of Quebec's first bishop. He sneaked in an hour's rest before heading to a mass attended by at least 200,000 people at Laval Stadium. All this followed an eight-hour flight from Rome.

John Paul was quick to begin spreading his central message – that faith must be cherished, that Catholics must find a way to mix "the modernity of America" with the deep-seated traditions of humanity. "Do not accept a divorce between faith and culture," he told those at the Laval mass. "You are being called at the present time to a new missionary effort."

The stately pomp of the service, the flowing white and gold robes of the Pope and attendant bishops, contrasted with the informal garb of the congregation. Many in the crowd spreading out in waves from the pyramidal altar wore jeans and T-shirts, sun-dresses and casual clothes.

Ste-Anne-de-Beaupré, Trois-Rivières

People pull on the Pope's robe as he moves through the crowd at Ste-Anne-de-Beaupré. (Andy Clark/UPC/CP)

Aboriginal woman presents John Paul with a prayer shawl in Ste-Anne-de-Beaupré. (Andy Clark/UPC/CP) ▶

Day Two: September 10, 1984

There are two hauntingly Catholic places in Canada, both built by Jesuits and memorable for their striking physical presence, their significance in the history of the church in Canada and as places where miracles are believed to happen. One is Ste-Anne-de-Beaupré northeast of Quebec City. It's one of the first French settlements in North America, the first shrine in North America and also the largest shrine in the world dedicated to Christ's grandmother, the patron saint of Quebec. The other is the Martyrs' Shrine near Georgian Bay in Ontario, Canada's national shrine to the eight Jesuits, including Father Jean de Brébeuf, who were slain 350 years ago. Both churches were on John Paul's 1984 itinerary, and he used them as backdrops to introduce the thorny topic of aboriginal self-government to his tour.

Under a leaden sky at Ste-Anne-de-Beaupré, he spoke in defence of aboriginal rights to about 12,000 people, many of them representing Canada's ten major aboriginal groups. The Pope lamented the poverty and discrimination that tainted native lives in Canada. "You must be the architects of your own future, freely and responsibly," he said. But he stopped short of advocating aboriginal self-government, evoking mixed responses from leaders hoping to hear a more affirmative statement. The crowd's response to the Pope's speech was warmest when he spoke phrases in aboriginal languages or mentioned Kateri Tekakwitha, the Mohawk born in 1656 who was beatified by John Paul in 1980. She died at age 24, having dedicated her life to charitable works. Her statue sits in a niche on the exterior of the church and is visited regularly by pilgrims.

After the Pope spoke, he walked through the crowd and many grabbed his white robe to make him stop longer. One small girl threw her arms around his neck and clung there determinedly for a minute before he could break free. When the Pope was presented with a leather stole appliquéd with pictures of canoes and whales from the East Coast Mi'kmaq, John Paul

◄ Pope John Paul II meets young member of aboriginal community in Ste-Anne-de-Beaupré. (Andy Clark/UPC/CP)

Many hands reach out to greet the Pope in Ste-Anne.
▼ (Gianni Foggia/CP)

Another young aboriginal baby gets some attention
▼ from the Pope. (Vatican Pool/CP)

immediately removed the crimson stole from around his neck and replaced it with the gift.

From Ste-Anne, the Pope headed by Via train to Trois-Rivières, where about 100,000 people had waited hours to see him, despite rain and cold weather. He travelled by popemobile to nearby Cap-de-la-Madeleine, best known to Catholics as the site in 1888 where the eyes of a statue of the Virgin reportedly opened for several minutes. Here he spoke at an open-air mass to a crowd of about 50,000. Many of the 600 priests who assisted him with the mass wore yellow rain slickers and plastic bags on their heads in an attempt to shield themselves from the weather.

Then it was back on board the train to return to Montreal. "Frequency: Once in a Lifetime" was what 40 select Via Rail employees read on their time sheets after they were chosen for the ride through the scattered communities along the St. Lawrence River. Despite a constant drizzle, thousands of Quebecers lined up in cornfields and roadsides, on rooftops and in clutches at railway crossings, to catch a glimpse of the 10-car train. Some were standing on the wrong side of the tracks, while the Pope looked the other way. For those who saw him, he was only a blur but they waved anyway.

Pope John Paul II blesses the crowd at a mass in ▶
Jarry Park, Montreal on Sept. 11, 1984.
(Ron Poling/UPC/CP)

Montreal

Day Three: September 11, 1984

Three days, three masses. The Pope's schedule was brutal by any definition, but his endurance was one of the traits most admired by Catholics. John Paul spent his third day in Canada's second-largest city and it was another 12-hour-plus feat. He started out with a visit to the tomb of Brother André, a Quebecer reputed to have performed miracle cures around 1900 who was beatified by John Paul in 1982. Then, at St. Joseph's Oratory atop Mount Royal, he gave what amounted to a pep talk to about 3,000 priests. Stand firm in your faith, he told them. Reject materialism. Réjean Martin, a 26-year-old seminarian, said the pontiff's visit would "put all the dynamism that used to exist back into the church."

▲ Quebec Premier René Lévesque and John Paul arrive at the Museé du Québec. (Jacques Nadeau/CP)

Also on the agenda was the beatification of Mother Marie-Léonie Paradis at the largest gathering yet of his tour — a mass for more than 300,000 at Jarry Park. The choice of Mother Marie-Léonie, who founded the Little Sisters of the Holy Family, was controversial. Canadian bishops had not been consulted and the move was criticized by Quebec

Perhaps in reaction to the criticism, the Pope lavished praise several times in Montreal on two other pioneering Catholic women: Marguerite Bourgeoys, the 17th-century founder of the Mother House of the Sisters of the Congregation in Montreal and the first Canadian woman to be named a saint; and Sister Catherine of St. Augustine, who founded Quebec's

"This woman is one of you, humble among the humble, and today she takes her place among those whom God has lifted up to glory. I am happy that for the first time, this beatification is taking place in Canada, her homeland."
-Pope John Paul II, at the beatification of Sister Marie-Léonie Paradis, Montreal, September 11, 1984

women upset that the Pope, in the first beatification in North America, had chosen to recognize a woman for her role as a helpmate to men — the order is known primarily for its domestic and secretarial service to priests.

first hospital in the 17th century. During mass, the Pope praised the contribution of religious communities run by women in Canada. In a forceful voice that echoed throughout the sports stadium, he seemed to suggest that men and women have different roles

The hand of a child reaches out to touch the Pope as he walks through a crowd of children at Montreal's Notre Dame Cathedral. (Fred Chartrand/CP)

to play within the church. Some, including Archbishop Joseph-Aurèle Plourde of Ottawa, interpreted his comments to mean that church work traditionally performed by women should not be considered inferior. But others, including Sister Mary Jo Leddy of Toronto, a prominent Catholic activist, thought the Pope had ignored subjects of importance to women, not just ordination but work and family issues.

Later, about 2,600 singing, dancing, laughing and sometimes weeping children gave the Pope his most boisterous and emotional welcome yet at Notre Dame Basilica in old Montreal. "*Vive le pape,*" the children, aged 10 and 11, cried as he waded though a sea of outstretched hands, kissing foreheads, patting cheeks, receiving gifts of books and Bibles and exchanging whispered confidences that moved many, children and parents alike, to tears. At times the Pope appeared as spellbound as the youngsters by the highly dramatic encounter.

The Pope is surrounded by school children at Notre Dame Cathedral. (Andy Clark/UPC/CP)

▲ Pope John Paul II holds hands with some children at Notre Dame Cathedral. (Gianni Foggia/CP)

The Pope is surrounded youthful followers at a rally in St. John's. ▶ (Jim Mone/CP)

But the day was still not over. That night, the Pope joined about 65,000 young people at a song-and-dance rally at Olympic Stadium. In a forerunner to the Pope's World Youth Days, the teens had come from all over Quebec and even Labrador, and slept on gymnasium floors or were billeted in Catholic homes. There was a choreographed welcome of 700 girls dressed in flowing white who formed the shape of a dove on the stadium field to symbolize peace, while musical themes addressed such issues as war, pollution, unemployment and the "true meaning of life."

Newfoundland

Day Four: September 12, 1984

The tiny outport of Flatrock on the Atlantic coast north of St. John's, Newfoundland, doesn't get into the news much. When it does, it is often for something bad — a deadly fire, or the wicked weather that haunts the Newfoundland coast. But in 1984, John Paul brought the world to Flatrock, then a totally Catholic community of 935 souls. Even though the population doubled for the Pope's visit, it was still one of the smallest crowds that the Pope addressed in his Canadian tour. His visit here had an

> "Young people are hungry today for truth and justice because they are hungry for God."
> *-Pope John Paul II, St. John's, Newfoundland, September 12, 1984*

intimacy not present in other communities, despite the presence of hundreds of police officers – almost overpowering in a community that didn't have a police station normally.

ciple of Christ, said the fishing industry was becoming too concentrated and risked being "controlled by the profit motive of a few." He lamented the worldwide economic uncertainty that had led to high unemploy-

"Bless these men and women who earn their living from the sea. Bless these fishing boats and protect those who use them."

-Pope John Paul II, Flatrock, Newfoundland, September 12, 1984

He knew the concerns of his crowd, winning it over with a ringing attack on big fishing companies delivered with the enthusiasm of a trawlerman downing a Blue Star beer, as one observer put it. "He had a message for the fish companies, didn't he?" said a satisfied Norman Kielly, who made his living hauling cod from the sea. The Pope, considered by his church to be the successor of St. Peter, the fisherman and dis-

ment. "It is a cruel paradox that many of you who could be engaged in the production of food are in financial distress here, while at the same time hunger, chronic malnutrition and the threat of starvation afflict millions of people elsewhere in the world." He suggested fishing co-operatives, joint ownership between workers and management, even a restructuring of the entire economy to put people before profit.

The Pope blesses a fleet of fishing boats in Flatrock. (Peter Bregg/CP)
Far Left: The popemobile travels past a rural home en route to Flatrock. (Andy Clark/UPC/CP)

In the rocky harbour below the pavilion built specially for the Pope's visit, about four dozen fishing boats bobbed in the shape of a cross bent out of shape by a stiff seaborne wind. They had gathered to be blessed by the Pope – there were to have been more, but the rough September weather had kept them away.

The homey tone of the visit to Newfoundland continued later in St. John's, where John Paul met thousands of children, elderly people and the sick and handicapped, and celebrated mass for 80,000 at the foot of historic Signal Hill. There were jigs and reels played on fiddles and accordions, and step dancers clattered to the strains of "I'se the Bye," a traditional Newfoundland song.

But the Pope addressed some serious issues as well, telling St. John's educators that modern society should not abandon God "at the schoolhouse door" and that the state has a responsibility to help finance denominational schools. And at the mass near Quidi Vidi, he delivered a stern defence of traditional family values, a homily that did not sit well with everyone. "Feminists in the church, and that's a large group of people," said Sister Lorraine Michael, "are going to be concerned about the heavy use of sexist language in this particular homily."

The bad weather that was a feature on many stops on the Pope's tour followed him to mass in St. John's. "It is the third time during my visit to Canada that I am celebrating with rain," he said at the mass. The cold, wet weather, however, did not prevent 3,000 young people from greeting him at an evening rally, where the Pope tapped his foot to folk music and a spontaneous chorus of "Singin' in the Rain."

Newfoundland, New Brunswick, & Nova Scotia

Day Five: September 13, 1984

The official plan was to head straight to the airport to catch a flight to Moncton, New Brunswick. But the crew of a Polish schooner docked at St. John's harbour had its own plan – to wave down the Pope's limousine so they could meet him. The Gedania had been built in the Gdansk shipyard that gave birth to the outlawed Solidarity trade union movement and its crew were the sons and daughters of Gdansk shipyard workers. Although Captain Wojtek Wierzbicki, the Gedania's skipper, had been ordered by the Polish government to stay away from the Pope during his Canadian visit, he found the temptation to meet a fellow countryman known for his fight against Communism was too great. When the horns of a nearby sealing vessel blasted, signalling the Pope's arrival, the young sailors, clad in orange and yellow rain gear, unfurled their banner in the pouring rain and the limo pulled over. They leaned into the back seat to receive a kiss and blessing from the Pope. "I feel good because . . . I used this chance," said Wierzbicki. "We are Catholics and every time we can possibly see John Paul, that is good for us."

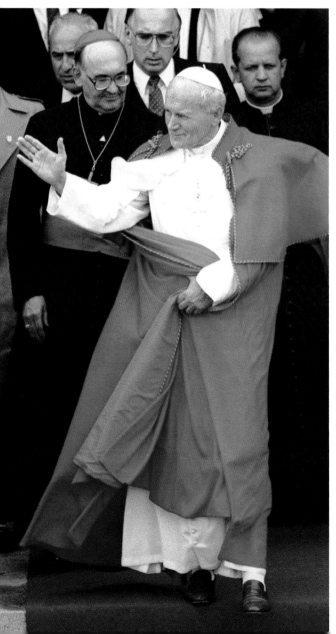

◄ John Paul leaves Our Lady of the Assumption Cathedral in Moncton, N.B. (Robert Kozloff/CP)

The Pope went back to his scheduled events, arriving to a wet but rousing welcome in New Brunswick, home to a large contingent of Catholics, mostly French-speaking Acadians. About 100,000 people thronged along his 12-kilometre motorcade route through the streets of Moncton to Our Lady of the Assumption Cathedral, where New Brunswick clergy had gathered. There, the Pope made a strong appeal for ecumenism, the ultimate unification of all Christian churches. "God wills that his people should live with a single heart and soul," he declared.

"Despite the trials of deportation and even the threat of annihilation because of political vicissitudes, the Acadians remained faithful to their faith, faithful to their culture, faithful to the land to which they continuously strove to return."
-*Pope John Paul II, Moncton, New Brunswick, September 13, 1984*

But it was his mention of the trials of the Acadians, who were forced out of the region in the 18th century by the British, that most moved his audience. He compared the age-old struggle of the Acadians to preserve their language and traditions to the fight in Poland against Soviet domination. "Despite the trials of deportation and even the threat of annihilation because of political vicissitudes, the Acadians remained faithful to their faith, faithful to their culture, faithful to the land," he said. The Pope's words were a resounding hit with his audience. Sister Marie Dorothe of Notre Dame de Sacre Coeur in Moncton described his comments as "perhaps the most

◄ Pope John Paul greets the crowd on his way to say mass on converted farmland in Moncton on Sept. 13. (Andy Clark/UPC/CP)

▲ About 200,000 people gather for the Moncton mass. (Morris Lamont/CP)

moving moment of my life." Said Rita Richardson of Rivière du Portage: "We didn't even know he knew about the Acadians in New Brunswick and for so long we've had quite a hard time keeping our culture and our language."

A crowd, meanwhile, had been building since 4 a.m. at a mass site near Magnetic Hill, an optical-illusion tourist attraction where cars appear to roll uphill. The group eventually comprised about 100,000 people, smaller than expected because of the rain, to hear the Pope reiterate his comments on the struggle of the Acadians. He celebrated the mass using a golden chalice given to Acadian bishops early in the 20th century by Pope Pius X.

Then it was on to Halifax, where the Pope finally lost the rain that had dogged his tour. At another youth rally of about 80,000, he stood in the glare of floodlights, waving to the cheering throng on the city's Commons, a sweeping expanse of lawn next to

Citadel Hill. As in his previous meetings with young people, the Pope told them they could help build a better world. "To the world of 1984 and beyond, to our families and to our cities, we must bring the gifts of communion and love," he said. "We must forge the bonds of justice and peace." He impressed many in the crowd. "The other popes kept quiet," said André Kelly. "They stayed over in the Vatican. John Paul comes to visit us. That's why I like him."

The Pope's day wasn't over yet. His final stop was at St. Mary's Basilica, where he told a group of lay ministers that their work was valued by the church. His last act of the day was unveiling a tablet commemorating the 200th anniversary of the Catholic Church in Halifax. By the end of his fifth day in Canada, John Paul had covered four provinces, including the most Catholic corners of the country – but the mammoth sweep of the land west of Quebec was still ahead of him.

▲ Toronto Archbishop Emmett Cardinal Carter greets the Pope as he arrives in Toronto on Sept. 14. (Vatican Pool/CP)

Nova Scotia & Ontario

Day Six: September 14, 1984

If anything, the already frenetic pace established by the Pope's tour of Canada seemed to speed up by the halfway point, when Day Six of the visit saw him start the day by celebrating mass with 120,000 people in Halifax, then end the day on Toronto's waterfront at a rally with 50,000 Polish-Canadians. In between, there were visits to a hospital, various churches and one city hall. And there were the usual popemobile motorcades, in two cities in different provinces. The Pope's schedule called for a break of about an hour for dinner and "rest" – the only time he was out of the public eye, other than the flight from Halifax to Toronto.

The mass on the Commons in Halifax was another rain-soaked event. The Pope paid homage to missionaries at the mass, noting that many Canadian ones had died carrying out their tasks in far-flung corners of the globe. He had preceded the mass with a quick visit to Izaak Walton Killam Hospital for children, where he blessed children and, in one case, a Cabbage Patch doll named Jennifer brought along by eight-year-old Robin Nickerson.

Later, in Toronto, he was back in his popemobile for a 12-kilometre drive through the streets to Nathan Phillips Square, site of City Hall. Tens of thousands of people, many waving papal flags and standing 20 deep in places, cheered the Pope along the route. Banks, stores and offices had been closed shortly before the procession began. Toronto's many Polish-Canadians were everywhere; they strung a Solidarity banner across the front doors

"The needs of the poor must take priority over the desires of the rich; the rights of workers over the maximization of profits; the preservation of the environment over uncontrolled industrial expansion; production to meet social needs over production for military purposes."

-*Pope John Paul II, Toronto, September 14, 1984*

of the Royal Ontario Museum and a six-piece band played Polish music. Souvenir salesmen stationed along the papal route, however, complained about a lack of business. Some lowered prices — papal banners dropped to $1.50 from $4 after the Pope's procession passed.

The Pope and Toronto Mayor Art Eggleton walk in the Peace ▶ Garden at City Hall. (Hans Deryk/CP)

After lighting an eternal flame at the newly constructed Peace Garden at Nathan Phillips Square, the Pope headed to the city's most prominent Roman Catholic church, St. Michael's Cathedral, a few blocks away, where he told more than 1,000 black-robed priests that their celibacy is a necessary component of their priestly role. While conceding that a priest's life can be lonely, discouraging and full of sacrifice, it is not possible to end the celibacy requirement, he said. "The heart of a priest, in order that it may be available for this service, must be free. Celibacy is a sign of a freedom that exists for the sake of service." Not all the priests were pleased by his address. "I don't agree the role of the clergy should be limited to the celibate," said Jim Sanford, a 28-year-old seminarian. "In the future we are going to need priests who are married and who have children."

While the Pope spoke in the cathedral, patrons at the nearby Silver Rail bar watched him on television. "It's quieter here than it's ever been before, probably in 90 years," said Al Cooper, who was nursing a drink and a cigar. "I'm not a Catholic but I like the fact that he

John Paul addresses clergy gathered at St. Michael's Cathedral. (Mike Blake/CP)

stands for a faith and delivers a message to young people that they need all over the world."

The Pope also squeezed in an ecumenical service at St. Paul's Anglican Church, urging, as he did in Flatrock, Newfoundland, big business to consider people above profits. The spectacle of a pope in an Anglican church showed some the Pope's spirit of ecumenism, but not all the Christian church leaders at the service were convinced by the image. Reverend Lois Wilson of the United Church of Canada and Bishop William Huras of

By far the most dramatic event of the day was the Polish rally at Toronto's Exhibition Place. Set against the backdrop of the Solidarity movement in Poland – its leader, Lech Walesa, had won the Nobel Peace Prize the year before for championing workers' rights – the Pope's support for the outlawed movement was greeted with roaring approval by the Poles assembled. It seemed a stretch of his own often-expressed rule that priests should not become actively involved in politics. Speaking in his native language, the Pope said

registered most deeply. "Seeing him tonight is like seeing family," said Andrew Czyszczon of Chicago. "We come from the same area in southern Poland. He used to go hiking in our area all the time and the stories he heard from the shepherds he used as parables when he was a priest." For a recently married Andrew Matyszewski of Toronto, the Pope's remarks on the family were most memorable. "It's really moving, I get goosebumps . . ." he said. "It's just a funny feeling. You see other people, other dignitaries, the prime minister. I don't feel the

"I hope that you young men and women will remain true to yourselves and that you will be able to rediscover the heritage that has been transmitted to you by your parents."
-Pope John Paul II, Toronto, September 14, 1984

the Lutheran Church both noted that the Catholic Church is not part of the Canadian or world councils of churches, which most other Christian faiths support as a proponent of Christian unity. They also noted that the Pope had not mentioned the leaders of non-Christian religions in his audience.

continued struggle by Poles will help "achieve this desire of being ourselves . . . living our own life, as Polish citizens." Some of the remarks were not part of a prepared text released before the address.

But for many of the Polish-Canadians and Americans at the rally, the Pope's endorsement of Solidarity was not the message that

same." At the end of the evening, which was brisk and cold at the waterfront stadium, the Pope and the crowd sang a hymn in Polish. Members of the choir – clad in light summer outfits – dashed off-stage between numbers to huddle away from the wind and blow on their hands.

▲ The Pope sits at the altar of the mass site in Downsview on Sept. 15, 1984. (Luciano Mellace/CP)

Ontario

Day Seven: September 15, 1984

A dream that began hundreds of years ago at the Jesuit mission of Ste-Marie-Among-the-Hurons on Georgian Bay finally came true with Pope John Paul's arrival. Jean de Brébeuf, a Jesuit from France, had died a martyr in the bush at the hands of the Iroquois in 1649, after a ten-year effort to bring the Roman Catholic faith to the aboriginal people living in the wilderness of Huronia. Pope John Paul, under considerably less arduous circumstances, celebrated that faith with 100,000 pilgrims – including many aboriginals – 335 years later.

The Martyrs' Shrine, the first place of pilgrimage ever designated in North America, pays tribute to Brébeuf and seven other "blackrobes" also named saints for their missionary efforts: Isaacs Jogues, Charles Garnier, Anthony Danile, Gabriel Lallemant, Noel Chabanel, John de Lalande and Rene Goupil. Their pioneering work is further commemorated in the nearby fort of Ste-Marie-Among-the-Hurons. For these 17th-century Jesuits, getting to Huronia from the established settlement of Quebec was a long journey by canoe, filled with dangers and discomforts. The Pope arrived in the area, still surrounded by wooded hills, by helicopter from Toronto in under an hour, although it could be suggested that his

visit to Ontario – containing, as it did, ten major events in 40 hours – required stamina similar to that needed by the early missionaries.

Looking well-rested, the pontiff greeted an enthusiastic crowd in the nearby town of Midland before briskly travelling four kilometres in his popemobile to the replica of the 17th-century Huron village. Then he headed to the shrine, where the sick and elderly waited to meet him. He lingered several minutes to console them before his address.

"Here the first Christians of Huronia found a house of prayer and a home of peace … and here today stands the Martyrs' Shrine, a symbol of hope and faith, a symbol of the triumph of the cross," John Paul said as he stood by a pine altar near the double-spired shrine at the site first seen by French explorer Samuel de Champlain in 1610.

Smoke from the fragrant sweetgrass, an aboriginal symbol of purity, wafted from the altar during a special ceremony in which First Nations communities from across Ontario offered the Pope an eagle feather, a sign of knowledge and courage. "It meant

Pope John Paul II | 51

so much to touch him," said Carol Jones, an Ojibwa woman who scrambled under barricades and pushed through the crowd to reach the Pope.

John Paul's words were mild compared with those he made earlier at the Quebec shrine in Ste-Anne-de-Beaupré, where he told aboriginal representatives that they must be "architects of your own future." Instead, the pontiff praised the courage of the martyrs, the legacy of aboriginal culture and urged greater aboriginal participation in the church. He hailed the First Nations' "sense of gratitude for the land, their responsible stewardship of the earth, their reverence for all His great works, their respect for their elders."

Back in Toronto, meanwhile, hundreds of thousands of people were gathering at a former military base for the visit's largest event, an afternoon mass for upwards of 300,000 people that was part spiritual event, carnival midway, military manoeuvre and media extravaganza. The weather was cold and windy, the grounds damp and swampy enough that some sank knee-deep in bog. Many thinly dressed worshippers were treated for hypothermia by first-aid attendants. When the Pope's helicopter

▲ The eagle feather ceremony continues. (Andy Clark/UPC/CP)

landed from Midland, treasured papal commemorative caps worn by volunteers went flying across the muddy parking lots. With souvenir hunters in hot pursuit of the caps and children chasing the popemobile as if it were an ice-cream truck, the moment took on the air of a country fair.

The event produced other unorthodox moments. Photographers eagerly snapped away as lines of vestment-clad priests queued up outside of the thousands of portable toilets, or "vati-cans," as some were calling them. More than 1,200 priests distributed communion to the crowds and, at the end of the mass, a van travelled

the area with volunteers collecting the unused hosts in green garbage bags.

Pope John Paul told the mud-splattered worshippers that all segments of society needed to unite to ensure that technology would serve, rather than impoverish, humankind. "The same technology that has the possibility to help the poor sometimes even contributes to poverty, limits the opportunities for work and removes the possibility of human creativity," the Pope said, as his silken overgarment flapped unmanageably in the strong winds. Prime Minister John Turner was among those served communion by the Pope at the mass.

The Pope holds an eagle feather given to him by First Nations ▶ people. The feather is considered the highest honour bestowed upon someone. (Andy Clark/UPC/CP)

"This is truly the hour for Canadians to heal all the divisions that have developed over the centuries between the original peoples and the newcomers to this continent. This challenge touches all individuals and groups, all churches and ecclesial communities throughout Canada. Once again in the words of St. Paul: "Now is the favourable time; this is the day of salvation."

-Pope John Paul II, Midland, September 15, 1984

Many among the crowd at the mass said they were glad they got a chance to see the Pope, but would think twice before going through the aggravation again. Even some of the 8,000 volunteers, some of whom worked at the site for upwards of 50 hours, were less than delighted with the experience. "A lot of volunteers want to go home," said one. "They are so mad at the organizers they won't even speak to them. They stayed here in the end because of the Pope."

John Paul then visited the construction site of the Byzantine Slovak Cathedral, the first to be built in the Americas. The Byzantine Slovak faith has often been considered on the fringes of Catholicism – it allows its priests to be married, for example – and the Pope's stop at the cathedral site was widely interpreted as an attempt by the Vatican to build bridges to that community. Speaking in Slovakian to about 20,000 people, he expressed the hope that Christ would "hasten a time of peace and total freedom for the church in the land of your origin."

Later, at his final event of the day at the Metropolitan Toronto Convention Centre, the Pope met laymen who had helped organize his tour. His public day ended 12 hours after it began, when he returned to the Rosedale residence of Emmett Cardinal Carter, Archbishop of Toronto, for the night.

John Paul waves to the estimated 400,000 persons gathered at Downsview Park for mass. (Pool/CP)

A group of young women in traditional Ukrainian dress surround the Pope outside Saints Vladimir and Olga Cathedral in Winnipeg. (Jose More/CP)

Manitoba & Alberta

Day Eight: September 16, 1984

Pope John Paul began his visit to Canada's West much like his other stops — by demonstrating his touch for the simple gesture that made him so popular. Ignoring the wishes of his security people, he crossed the tarmac at the Canadian Forces airport in Winnipeg to meet delighted fans and bless some children. "Whenever there are people around, this just seems to create new energies and he just revels in that," commented Archbishop Adam Exner, one of three

Winnipeg archbishops who were trying to keep the pontiff on schedule.

Winnipeg was John Paul's kind of town, a place where he could speak in Ukrainian as a "fellow Slav," as he put it in an appearance at Saints Vladimir and Olga Ukrainian Catholic Cathedral. Winnipeg showed its appreciation, honouring the Pope with a St. Boniface General Hospital Research Foundation award for his defence of human rights and freedom. The award has also been given to Mother Teresa.

But it wasn't just Winnipeggers who gathered in Manitoba's largest city to catch a sight of the Pope. Among the 200,000 people at Birds Hill Park for the afternoon mass were many who drove hundreds of kilometres from other parts of Manitoba, Ontario, Saskatchewan and neighbouring U.S. states. Lillian Dupuis of Rivers, Manitoba, and her four children camped overnight outside the site. She said she was trying to teach her children "to put God first, which is against the norm." Others were not even Catholic but were attracted by the pomp and circumstance surrounding the Pope. "We do have a moderator, but it's not the same," said Jeff Hunter, a member of the United Church of Canada. Kaushik Parasnis, a student from India, said he and his three companions, none of them Christians, were attracted for another reason. "I wanted to experience the frenzy of the people, rather than the mass itself."

There was no rain, unlike previous outdoor masses, but a brisk prairie wind continually mussed the pontiff's thinning hair and aides had to hold onto his robes to keep them from flapping about uncontrollably. In his homily, the Pope called for tolerance of ethnic minorities. "The best interests of justice are served by those public authorities who do all they can to improve the human conditions of the members of ethnic minorities, especially in what concerns their language, culture, customs and their economic activity and enterprises," he said, quoting one of his predecessors, Pope John XXIII.

Two hours later he was in a limousine, heading back to the airport to continue his journey to Edmonton. Alberta had planned an elaborate welcome, with about 40 ethnic groups performing on stages along his 15-kilometre motorcade route from the airport to St. Joseph's Basilica. Now about 30 minutes behind schedule, the popemobile sailed by the stages rapidly in the gathering dusk, giving the Pope little opportunity to see and hear the colour, music and dance that had been arranged for him.

As had happened elsewhere, hordes of people began to gather for the next day's mass, this one at the Namao Armed Forces base, even as the Pope continued his schedule elsewhere. While he held a prayer service at the basilica that evening, overnight campers at the mass site were entertained on a giant screen with religious movies such as *Shoes of the Fisherman* and *The Agony and the Ecstasy*. Frank Greschuk, 68, arrived with his 67-year-old wife from Innisfree, Alberta., and settled in for a 20-hour wait. "It's a once-in-a-lifetime experience, a pleasure to see the Pope," said Greschuk, a Catholic, adding that his only reservation was being seated beside one of the many young children spending the night in a stroller. The mass site had the air of a carnival midway. Food concessions with flashing lights and names such as Wild Bill's Canteen and Fat Freddy's offered hotdogs, perogies and pizza.

Alberta

Day Nine: September 17, 1984

Before he boarded a helicopter to head to the Edmonton mass site, the Pope met seven children who had won a newspaper essay contest. It was an intimate gathering, which the later mass could not be, but John Paul showed his ability at handling both types of encounters. He greeted and blessed each child individually, with the most touching moment coming when he met Ronny Gonzalez, 12, of Edmonton, whose father was in a Chilean jail for political crimes. The pontiff embraced and kissed the stunned youngster, telling him to "have faith" in his father's future. Another student, Debbie Davis, 17, of Red Deer, Alberta, had asked the Pope in her essay why women weren't allowed to be Catholic priests. She might have disagreed with his politics, but she complimented the Pope on his people skills. "He comes down to your level — he doesn't act like he's above you," she said after meeting him.

▲ Pope John Paul (at bottom of steps) is led to the altar by other members of the clergy as he prepares to say mass near Edmonton. (Dave Buston/CP)

By the time of the mass, an estimated 125,000 had gathered to hear a thunderous homily from the Pope that denounced the developed world of the Northern Hemisphere for its treatment of the South. Hands flying, his voice rising to a booming pitch, his robes billowing in the wind on the altar 47 steps up from canopy soaring over the altar like a giant white dove, had an evangelistic element, a grander take on the religious revival meetings of the Dirty '30s, when itinerant preachers took to the dusty back roads in the West and elsewhere, attracting crowds with their promises of a better world. "I wanted to be an itinerant catechist,"

> "The poor people and poor nations – poor in different ways, not only lacking food, but also deprived of freedom and other human rights – will judge those people who take these goods away from them, amassing supremacy at the expense of others."

> "Today we are praying in Canada, in the city of Edmonton, for the progress of peoples."

> *-Pope John Paul II, Edmonton,*
> *September 17, 1984*

the crowd, he tried to make the plight of the Southern Hemisphere something the rest of the world cared about. "The poor people and poor nations . . . will judge those people who take these goods away from them, amassing supremacy at the expense of others."

The Edmonton mass, held on a vast, flat plain surrounding a magnificent podium with a surrealistic John Paul had said earlier in his life. "One who can hand on the Christian faith and make it intelligible and attractive to all people." The winds tearing across the field sent many running for cover but scarcely affected the thrill of the occasion for others. "The man is a holy man and it inspires people to take a new look at their lives," said Bob Forest of Edmonton.

After the afternoon mass, the Pope was scheduled to have his first real rest of the tour, at the Marmot Basin ski resort in Jasper National Park. But the gusting winds that lent such drama to the mass grounded the helicopter that was to have taken him there. He was whisked initially to Government House, the wood-panelled mansion once inhabited by Alberta's lieutenant-governors, and then to Elk Island National Park, about 35 kilometres east of Edmonton, for some solitary hiking. The park doesn't offer glimpses of elk and grizzly bears as Jasper does, but is home to one of the largest captive populations of wood buffalo in the world, as well as beaver and other animals. The workers at Elk Island were surprised by the last-minute visit of the world's top Catholic, but apparently he wasn't hard to entertain. "We heard some reports that he had gone to the buffalo paddocks," said Don Bates in the park's pro shop. "And we had some wardens come up to get some food for him, some bran muffins."

Northwest Territories & British Columbia

Day Ten: September 18, 1984

Troubles began early for John Paul as he prepared to leave Edmonton for a key element in his Canadian tour, a three-hour stop in the aboriginal community of Fort Simpson, Northwest Territories, about 500 kilometres south of the Arctic Circle. First, he was forced to switch planes after a small fuel leak was discovered in the original aircraft. Then fog prevented his plane from landing in Fort Simpson and it had to head to Yellowknife to wait for better weather. But the fog didn't lift all that day, and Fort Simpson's loss was Yellowknife's gain.

The aboriginals in fogbound Fort Simpson, many of whom had travelled hundreds of kilometres by plane, boat or car, waited in vain in the cold, praying and chanting. Spiritual ceremonies had already been going on for three days, and preparations for the Pope much, much longer. Sonny McDonald of Fort Smith, N.W.T., had spent 100 hours constructing the chair, made of moose antlers and strips of caribou hide, the Pope was to sit on. McDonald just shook his head sadly when the word went out that the Pope wasn't going to get there.

▲ The Pope talks to aboriginal leaders Harry Daniels, left, who gave his traditional jacket to the Pope, and Francois Paulette, right of Daniels. (Staff/CP)

In Yellowknife, meanwhile, word spread quickly that the mining town was getting an unexpected visitor. A Mountie phoned his wife. The wife told her friend. Somebody else heard it on the radio. "Get down to the airport," said the message. "The Pope is dropping in."

By the time the Pope got off the plane, cheering people lined the chain-link fence around the tiny Yellowknife airport. A determined John Paul was escorted into the airport terminal where he videotaped his statement for later broadcast to those gathered at Fort Simpson. The message was a politically charged defence of native self-government, a plea for the provision of sufficient land and resources for aboriginal people, and an apology for "whatever mistakes were made" by the church's missionaries.

Once he finished his statement, the pontiff strolled through the airport lobby and out the back door to meet the hundreds who had gathered.

"I meet all of you here in Yellow?" asked the Pope. "Knife," answered the crowd in chorus.

Just an hour earlier, Harry Daniels, the flamboyant vice-president of the Native Council of Canada, had sat disconsolately in the airport coffee shop, frustrated that his own flight to Fort Simpson had been fogged in. Daniels now stripped off his trademark moose hide and beadwork jacket and presented it to John Paul. The planned presents for the pontiff were stranded in Fort Simpson. "We didn't have any presents here, so I thought I'd better give him one," Daniels said. All in all, the Yellowknife visit had an air of spontaneity that was lacking in many of the heavily orchestrated events on the tour. The Pope even added an off-the-cuff modification to his usual blessing, congratulating people "for having found the Pope . . . here in this airport."

In Fort Simpson, meanwhile, the disappointment was perhaps tempered by the Pope's message, which echoed many of the aboriginal leaders' demands from

The Pope displays a talking stick he was given by the Salish Nation in Vancouver. The stick indicates an elder's right to speak. (Jim Mone/CP)

▲ John Paul greets child in Yellowknife on Sept. 18. (Staff/CP)

governments. "I think he has indicated to the Canadian public and the world at large that he is indeed on our side," said Daniels.

Although organizers told the disappointed aboriginal community that they would try to rearrange the Pope's schedule to get him to the North, "even if he has to get up at 3 or 4 a.m.," it was not to happen. By the afternoon, the tightly scheduled tour had resumed its original agenda, with a papal mass at the airport in Abbotsford, British Columbia. Worshippers and celebrity buffs were decked out in baseball caps, straw hats and makeshift shields as the sun finally shone on the Canadian papal tour. An estimated 185,000 people heard the Pope's homily that encouraged British Columbians to tackle "the social problems that have become so much a part of the fabric of life in these parts" – which seemed a reference to the high unemployment, labour strife and widespread opposition to government austerity measures that were then bedevilling the province.

▲ John Paul at a celebration of life ceremony in Vancouver where he met young and old people of different ethnic backgrounds. (Joe Marquette/CP)

▲ The Pope accepts a talking stick from John L. George, an elder of the Salish Nation. (Gianni Foggia/Pool/CP)

The mass, as earlier ones did, attracted many of the Pope's countrymen, who waved red and white Polish flags and banners for Solidarity, the then-outlawed union movement in Poland. Many were jumpers – people who had left their ships while in

in Vancouver, the Pope minced no words in a condemnation of abortion, which he said "sets the stage for despising, negating and eliminating the life of adults and for attacking the life of society." It was the first time he had used the word abortion during the

> "If the weak are vulnerable from the time of conception, then they are vulnerable in old age and they are vulnerable before the might of an aggressor and the power of nuclear weapons."
>
> *Pope John Paul II, Vancouver, September 18, 1984*

port in Canada to seek political asylum. "He allows us to keep our roots, our heritage," said Christopher Korczak, who had come to Canada after being imprisoned in Poland for Solidarity activities. "He makes us believe that we are a community that has value – not just poor immigrants thrown out of our country."

Later, after a boisterous welcome at an evening service in the cavernous B.C. Place Stadium

Canadian tour and he chose to do it in the province with the highest abortion rate in the country. John Paul also urged wide-eyed schoolchildren not to be tempted by drugs, alcohol or materialism. He told the elderly in the crowd of about 60,000 that their experience and insight are needed. He told the disabled that the church wants them to take their rightful place in society.

▲ The Pope is hugged by children at Ottawa airport. (Vatican Pool/CP)

Ottawa-Hull

Day Eleven: September 19, 1984

◀ Clockwise from left: John Paul greets people at the airport in Ottawa. (Andy Clark/UPC/CP)
On the Rideau Canal in Ottawa. (Michel Tessier/CP)
Prime Minister Brian Mulroney and the Pope chat at Government House reception. (Ron Poling/UPC/CP)

The Pope spent much of his 11th day in Canada in the air, travelling from the West Coast to the country's capital. He wasn't in the public eye until late afternoon, but the hoopla that greeted his arrival more than made up for the absence earlier in the day. After arriving at Canada Forces Base Uplands, he was greeted by Canada's new prime minister, Brian Mulroney (who hadn't been sworn in when the Pope arrived 11 days earlier), camera-toting priests, 125 singers from a group called Up With People and hordes of children who squealed with delight and gave him flowers. Then the church bells began pealing as he began a ride down the Rideau Canal in a specially built "pope-boat" decked with flowers. A convoy of police in motorboats trailed him, while cyclists on nearby bike paths tried to keep pace with the flotilla. Children scrambled up trees along the canal for a better look, while others simply stepped out of their

The Pope's entourage moves down the Rideau
Canal in Ottawa on Sept. 19. (Staff/CP)

▲ John Paul arriving at Ottawa airport. (Andy Clark/UPC/CP)

office buildings for a glimpse. Just to be safe, police divers had searched the murky canal waters earlier but apparently found nothing more threatening than an old bicycle and a baby stroller.

The Pope's first public words of the day were a pep talk to nuns at the Convent of the Servants of Jesus-Mary in Hull. He said that although some might call the lives of nuns "foolishness," he urged them to continue their work despite the "weariness, routine and monotony" of their existence. "Your choice amazes, questions, interests or irritates the world, but it never leaves it indifferent." After mass with the cloistered nuns at the austere convent, the Pope's next stop was quite a contrast. Glittering Rideau Hall, home of Canada's Governor General, was filled with politicians, judges and diplomats from about 75 countries, with tickets to the most popular event in town – an audience with the Pope. John Paul, ever the savvy politician, took full advantage of the opportunity.

The Pope's entourage moves down the Rideau Canal past the Parliament Buildings. (Steve Pyle/CP)

In an address that tied together the several themes of his tour, he said society remained insensitive to some of the world's most deep-seated ills, including hunger, arms buildup, experimentation with human embryos, constraints on religious freedoms and the lack of basic health care for billions. But he added he had seen progress on the long road toward a society based on human values. He also praised Canada for its peace efforts, its contributions to projects

" I appeal to you today, and through you to all the people whom you represent, to be the bearers of a new vision of humanity: a vision that does not see society's problems in terms of economic, technical or political equations alone, but in terms of living people."

-Pope John Paul II, Ottawa, September 19, 1984

in the developing world and its generosity to refugees.

After his speech, the Pope went through a receiving line, meeting many of the politicians. It was his only significant encounter with politicians during his entire tour, much of which had been focused on large-scale masses and rallies with such groups as the young, the old and the handicapped.

The Pope waves to the crowd at Ottawa airport just before he leaves for Rome. (Above: Fred Chartrand/CP; below: Peter Bregg/CP)

Goodbye to Canada

Day Twelve: September 20, 1984

John Paul reserved a good chunk of his final day in Canada for a meeting with his "board" – the bishops in charge of the Canadian branch of the Catholic Church. While tens of thousands gathered for the afternoon mass that would be his last big event of the trip, the Pope met with the church's top officials for about three hours after a ceremony thanking organizers for their work on the tour. His message to his lieutenants in the church was straightforward and unbending: keep the faith, remain the guides of conscience for church members and, above all, don't let the "behaviour of the

world" influence church teachings. The meeting was not open to the public, but the Pope released a text of his presentation and several bishops spoke later about it. Bishop John O'Mara of Thunder Bay, Ontario, said the meeting was "rather formal" and dealt at length with John Paul's views on family life and the role of the priesthood as well as housekeeping and bureaucratic matters. On specific issues, he called for strict adherence to the church's positions on premarital sex and contraception. Apparently, he gave bishops two thumbs up on their running of the Canadian Catholic Church, even though the Canadian Conference of Catholic Bishops has a history of being more relaxed on issues such as birth control. In a 1968 document, the conference told Catholics they should be guided by informed conscience on the matter of contraception. Bishop Gerard Dionne of New Brunswick said he did not think the Pope's remarks on the subject during the meeting were a condemnation of the 1968 document, although "he did reaffirm the position of *Humanae Vitae*, the encyclical in which Pope Paul VI stated the Catholic position against artificial birth control."

Then, after this rather stern message, John Paul did what he did so well – went out and inspired a field full of people who, while they might have cheerfully ignored him on such personal issues as birth control, applauded him and loved him for his stand on peace and justice. During his final mass in Canada, for 250,000 people on a damp,

"Materialism can only question, diminish, trample underfoot, destroy, shatter that which is most profoundly human."

-Pope John Paul II, September 20, 1984

windswept plain on the banks of the Ottawa River, he called himself a "pilgrim of peace" and most of his comments addressed the evil of violence that threatened to "destroy all that is human." Yvon Lacoursière, 30, of Toronto said he shook when the Pope spoke of peace. "You can watch him on TV, but when you're actually there and see him, he sends shivers down your spine." The crowd applauded the Pope's emotional plea for peace eight times, accorded him a standing ovation and cried "Vive le Pape" once he finished, then kissed the altar and carried off its adornments after he left.

At 6:30 p.m. on September 20, the Pope's first visit to Canada and one of his most exhaustive foreign tours ended. He boarded his plane for Rome, but not before inviting himself back to Canada for a second visit, specifically to meet Canada's Aboriginal Peoples at Fort Simpson. About the tour, he said he could not "speak now of all that I will keep in my heart; that goes beyond what can be expressed in a few words."

The papal visit had totally absorbed Canada's media for 12 days and even prior to his visit, as newspapers and broadcasters provided their audiences with a steady diet of commentary on the state of the Roman Catholic Church in Canada, its history, its problems and its future. During the visit, there was dawn-to-dusk television coverage of every word the Pope uttered and every move he made. Despite this reliable coverage, hundreds of thousands still turned out, often in discouraging weather, to see him in person. The crowds were not always as huge as organizers had predicted but they were still larger than at any event in the country's history.

John Paul himself evoked cheers, weeping and sometimes skepticism, but rarely during the visit did he leave people indifferent. Canadians saw him in many roles – an Old Testament prophet, his robes flapping in the breeze; a Polish freedom fighter decrying tyranny; and a fatherly St. Nicholas clutching

> "I wish for the Canadian people a happy future, the development of all their qualities, a life lived in the harmony and respect for their cultural and spiritual difference."
> -Pope John Paul II, Ottawa, September 20, 1984

teary-eyed children to his chest. Sometimes his appearances could more appropriately be compared to that of a secular superstar. Canadians, even Catholics, might have had many issues with the Roman Catholic Church, its practices and its beliefs, but one thing was clear: John Paul II had a big fan club in Canada.

1987

Fulfilling a promise to Canada's Aboriginal Peoples

Pope John Paul II greets people, receives gifts from Dene Nation members. (From left, Chuck Stoody/CP; Chuck Stoody/CP; Dave Buston/CP)

The wait

They started coming to Fort Simpson, Northwest Territories, a few days before the Pope's arrival. The visitors, most of them members of the Dene Nation, trickled in from across the Northwest Territories, Yukon, British Columbia and the Prairies. Some spent their last dollars to charter planes or travel by boat from communities along the Mackenzie River. Some travelled hundreds of kilometres on buses. Many were elderly. About 5,000 people gathered for this visit – a far cry from the hundreds of thousands the Pope had drawn in other lands but an amazing number in Canada's far-flung, sparsely populated North.

The wait in Fort Simpson, a traditional gathering place for the indigenous peoples of Canada's North., actually started three years earlier. In 1984 fog had prevented the Pope's plane from landing in the community of 1,000. The area around Fort Simpson, where the Mackenzie and Laird rivers meet, is low-lying, and fog takes forever to clear once it creeps in. The Pope's schedule couldn't wait it out in 1984, and thousands of people were disappointed.

That wasn't going to happen in 1987 when the Pope, to keep his promise to the community, added Fort Simpson to the tail end of a gruelling trip to the United States. Just to be on the safe side, the Defence Department equipped his plane with radar, allowing it to fly even in poor visibility. And this time he had no commitments after his visit to the community, so he could wait around for weather to clear if necessary.

Fort Simpson had only one hotel, one motel and four restaurants, but a large campground first cleared in preparation for the 1984 visit was spruced up. Workers filled water barrels, chopped 100 cords of wood and set up hundreds of outhouses. The night before the Pope's arrival, the rhythmic tong-tong of drums and the chants of aboriginal singers interrupted the stillness of a starry

The Pope gives communion during mass in Fort Simpson. (Doug Ball/CP)

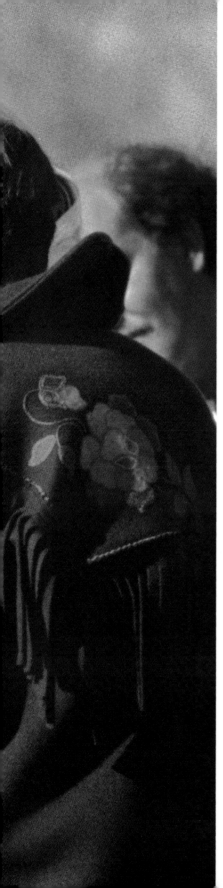

northern night. The air was filled with the sweet smell of burning pine and spruce, followed by the aroma of cooking caribou, moose, whitefish and bannock bread. The mood was one of quiet celebration – the Dene way, said Father George Posset, parish priest in Fort Providence, N.W.T. "I think it's a once-in-a-lifetime opportunity to see the Pope," said George Smith as he stood beside a crackling fire after travelling 2,000 kilometres from Pine House Lake, Saskatchewan. "He's our leader and I have great respect for the man. He's one of my heroes."

Native elders, who wanted the Pope's visit to be a spiritual event, had requested a ban on alcohol, drugs and gambling. "We have to make sure we don't make the same mistake we made in 1984, when we made it more of a carnival and political issue rather than a spiritual event," said Roy Fabien, a Dene from Hay River on Great Slave Lake.

But politics were hard to ignore. The Dene Nation had long fought for recognition from the Canadian government as a distinct group with the right to self-government. And the Pope was well-known for publicly

"Today I have come in order to assure you that the Church stands with you."
-Pope John Paul II, September 20, 1987

supporting aboriginal rights – he had spoken about the issue several times during the 1984 visit. A few days before his Fort Simpson visit, he apologized to Apaches in Arizona for some of the deeds of early missionaries.

Many Dene were hoping he would reiterate his support for aboriginal rights, although some were focused on other matters. Fabien made the trip for his parents – "it's a reward for their faith, for all the years they've followed the church" – and for his children. "The traditional ways of worshipping are all gone. We don't have anything else." Lorrina Pierrot, 17, had made the eight-hour drive with her family from Fort Resolution, N.W.T., because she hoped the gathering would strengthen the Dene culture. And some – like the elder who travelled 2,200 kilometres from Saskatchewan, had a simpler reason: "It's because I love the Pope."

The meeting

There was no fog, just morning rain and overcast skies that made for a damp wait for spectators. Then, moments before the Pope arrived, a rainbow arced across the Mackenzie River. "When it was announced the Pope's plane had landed, it brought a lump to my throat," said Harry Dickie, a former chief of the Fort Nelson band in British Columbia. "It's a once-in-a-lifetime thing to see a pope in the north country and we wanted to take advantage of it."

John Paul was welcomed to the community by Governor General Jeanne Sauvé, political leaders and elders who grinned at his arrival, as well as by children with gifts and flowers. He walked along the roped-off crowd, shaking hands, bending to stroke a grizzled cheek or kiss a child. The people, some in fringed deerskins with colourful embroidery, others in nylon windbreakers and baseball caps, reached out to touch him or speak a few words. Some stooped to kiss his ring. The crowd was almost silent, watching the man they call Yahtitah, the father of all priests. One elder held a battered tape recorder. Although he spoke no English, his son explained, he wanted to be able to hear the Pope's voice over and over.

The pontiff spent about 20 minutes talking privately with native leaders, while people filed by to present gifts of crafts, beadwork and leatherwork to his waiting aides. Then he spoke, from the shelter of a six-storey-high white teepee erected on a stage and

John Paul and Governor General Jean Sauvé meet. (Doug Ball/CP)

hood and sisterhood, to take more responsibility in the church. Four northern bishops assisted the Pope, who used a small gold chalice that had been used by Bishop Vital Grandin, the first bishop of Northern Canada, more than a century ago. The congregation seemed restless, but it may have been in keeping with northern informality.

"The soul of the native peoples of Canada is hungry for the spirit of God – because it is hungry for justice, peace, love, goodness, fortitude, responsibility and human dignity. This is indeed a decisive time in your history. It is essential that you be spiritually strong and clear-sighted as you build the future of your tribes and nations."

-Pope John Paul II, Fort Simpson, September 20, 1987

built of logs by local craftsmen. He said he came to the Aboriginal Peoples as a friend and as missionaries had done before him, to proclaim God's word. He spoke of the early missionaries, saying they respected native heritage, language and customs – comments that seemed in contrast with earlier statements and disappointed some members of his audience. Dene political leaders got their wish, however, when the Pope said they were entitled to self-government, as well as land and resources necessary to make it workable. "I pray that the Holy Spirit will help you all to find the just way so that Canada may be a model for the world in upholding the dignity of aboriginal peoples."

Later, during a mass that mixed native chants with the traditional Latin of the Catholic Church, the Pope called on young aboriginals to enter the priest-

It seemed to observers that John Paul took every opportunity to mingle with people. Margaret Kroskie, a Cree from Grande Prairie, Alberta, wasn't in a front row, but she reached out her hand and the Pope touched it. "My heart was pounding so hard it was almost like a current, an electrical current," she said. "It's a very emotional time for the Indian people."

Over it all throbbed the rhythmic, hypnotic beat of drums and the nasal chanting of aboriginal hymns. John Paul left Fort Simpson later that day, flying to Edmonton and then to Rome. After a wait of more than three years, his visit to Canada's North was over in five hours.

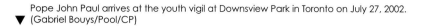
Pope John Paul arrives at the youth vigil at Downsview Park in Toronto on July 27, 2002.
▼ (Gabriel Bouys/Pool/CP)

2002
World Youth Day
and the Pope
come to Toronto

◀ A sea of young people almost surrounds the stage at the youth vigil.
(Frank Gunn/CP)

The welcome

On July 23, 2002, a fragile Pope John Paul set foot on Canadian soil for the first time in 15 years, braving more than two dozen steps down a steep airplane ramp with little more than a cane and a visibly nervous aide gripping his arm.

Prime Minister Jean Chrétien greets the Pope. (Kevin Frayer/CP)

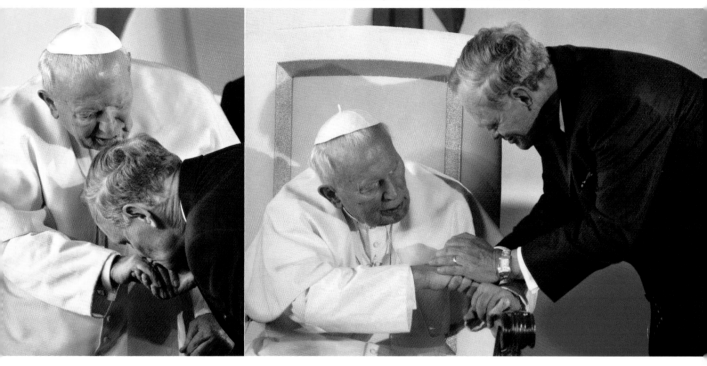

He surprised many when he walked down the stairs, ignoring the hydraulic lift hoisted nearby. Despite this impressive feat, he was still far different, physically, from the man who had visited Canada in the 1980s. Now in what even he called his "twilight years," the 82-year-old Pope was extremely fragile, a stooped figure suffering the ravages of Parkinson's disease as well as crippling knee and hip ailments. Once known for his skills as a communicator, he now found speech to be a challenge.

Pope John Paul II | 87

He was greeted by dignitaries, including Prime Minister Jean Chrétien, as well as some of the thousands of pilgrims gathering in Toronto for World Youth Day, begun by John Paul in 1986 as a festival of prayer and reflection for Catholic young people from around the world. Many erupted into tears. "It was very special to me," said Georgia Rae Giddings, a ten-year-old from Baysville, Ontario. "He's the closest one to God, and God is very special to me." Even Ontario Premier Ernie Eves admitted he was close to tears. "If you don't have a tingle in your spine and a tear in your eye, then you're not human. It really was a great emotional experience." The Pope was equally complimentary to Canada, calling it "a free, democratic and caring society, recognized throughout the world as a champion of human rights and human dignity."

◀ The Pope's motorcade winds its way to welcoming ceremonies at Exhibition Place, Toronto. (Aaron Harris/CP)

Although only a small group of people was permitted to attend the welcoming ceremony in an airport hangar, thousands of pilgrims from

"Canadians are heirs to an extraordinarily rich humanism, enriched even more by the blend of many different cultural elements."
                                                                    -Pope John Paul II, July 23, 2002

around the world gathered a few kilometres away at a downtown lakeside park to watch the Pope's arrival on an enormous television screen. The excitement in the air at Exhibition Park was palpable, with groups of young people breaking sometimes into song, sometimes into prayer. "We were told we didn't know if he was going to make it, so we had to pray for him, and now we're very excited to see he is here," said Chris Kulas, 23, who travelled for 18 hours in a bus from Galloway, Wisconsin, to attend the World Youth Day events.

Two pilgrims take part in World Youth Day ▶
activities at Exhibition Place. (Kevin Frayer/CP)

Pilgrims had to wait, however, to greet the Pope in person. He was immediately whisked away by a convoy of helicopters to a retreat belonging to the Basilian Fathers on Strawberry Island in Lake Simcoe, north of Toronto. After the nine-hour plane journey from Rome, the Pope enjoyed what was billed as his first vacation outside that city since becoming pontiff 24 years earlier. He seemed to enjoy the quiet time — he ventured out on the lake a couple of times, and during one boat tour made a surprise visit to a group of residents from a nearby home for the developmentally disabled.

◀ A young boy takes part in a ceremony unveiling at bronze sculpture of Pope John Paul by the Polish community in Brampton, Ont. (Kevin Frayer/CP)

The pilgrims

They came by plane, train and bus. Some slept in hotel beds, some on school gym floors. They invaded Toronto's streetcars and subways, streets and parks, singing and praying with such joy that even hardened city dwellers couldn't help but smile at their antics. The event was World Youth Day – and the draw was an 82-year-old man, stooped and frail, who described himself as "full of years but still young at heart."

The 400,000 or so pilgrims gathered at Toronto's Exhibition Park on July 25, 2002, gave Pope John Paul a raucous welcome befitting a pop star when they saw him for the first time in person. Clad in everything from shorts and T-shirts to robes and tunics, they had streamed all day long to the fairground, waving flags, singing and cheering. They danced, played guitars and tossed footballs and beach balls as they waited for the Pope's arrival.

Cheers rang out and tears flowed when he finally arrived and made his way, in his famous popemobile, slowly through the fairground to a massive stage built for the occasion. "John Paul II, we love you," the pilgrims cried out. He doffed his skullcap in greeting, smoothed his silver hair and formally welcomed Catholics from 170 countries. "My joyful and heartfelt greetings to you," he said

◀ Smile! A group of pilgrims from Pennsylvania record their visit to Toronto for World Youth Day. (Kevin Frayer/CP)

in muffled English. "The Pope, who loves you dearly, has come from afar to listen again with you to Jesus' words." The Pope's voice was slurred and difficult to understand, but the crowd listened with rapt attention. Many described the visit as life-altering. "When I come back to Montreal, I want to spread our love, spread our joy, spread everything the Pope just told us," said Justin Lee, 16.

The presentation also included a performance by the World Youth Day choir, comprising hundreds of young Ontario residents who spent two years preparing for the event. After the Pope gave a final blessing

"I commended you one by one in my prayers to the Lord. He has always known you, and he loves each one of you personally."

Pope John Paul II, July 25, 2002

and was taken by helicopter to the Strawberry Island retreat north of the city, hundreds of the pilgrims broke into an impromptu dance, singing joyously. Later, many, saying they were overwhelmed by the pontiff's speech, sat on the ground, hugging and crying, late into the night. Others celebrated, dancing in conga lines as musicians sang about their faith in a number of languages. Despite the fact the event drew nearly hundreds of thousands of young people, police had no serious problems, aside from the odd case of dehydration or a rambunctious pilgrim climbing a scaffold for a better view.

Elizabeth and Marie Hannah of Nashville, Tennessee join the crowd at Exhibition Place. (Kevin Frayer/CP)

Pope John Paul II | 95

▲ John Paul sits down for lunch with young Catholic pilgrims at a retreat on Strawberry Island. (Arturo Mari/Pool/CP)

Lunch with the Holy Father

The Pope invited 14 young people for lunch while he stayed at Strawberry Island on Lake Simcoe, and the experience left them singing as they returned by boat to the mainland. It was only a meal of spaghetti, asparagus and chocolate cake, but it created a memory to last a lifetime for the young people – three Canadians and one representative each from Germany, India, the United States, Sudan, China, Kenya, Australia, Peru, Jordan, Bosnia-Herzegovina and Tahiti-French Polynesia.

"It was very peaceful," said Emanuel Pires, 22, of Toronto. "Everyone kind of did their own thing from their country, whether dancing, singing or presenting something to him. He looked very happy. When we sang, sometimes he sang with us if he knew the words." Another Canadian pilgrim, Frank Sinclair of Toronto, had hardly slept the night before from excitement. Nothing in his life compared with the experience, he said. "I think it will be a while before it sinks in."

The Pope had spent part of the morning on a cruise of Lake Simcoe aboard the Blue Sapphire. Jim Ginou, owner of the 13-metre vessel, acted as skipper and host. "He drove down to the boat just to see it and instantly made the decision, 'I want to go on the boat,'" said Ginou, whose four sons acted as crew. "We put him on the back of the boat facing forward and we took the plastic (cover) down and we just drove around." One of Ginou's sons, Josh, 23, described the experience as surreal. "We're sitting in our family boat that we've had for 15 years and then you come up the steps and the Pope's just sitting there enjoying himself."

The vigil

One participant described the all-night vigil in Downsview Park before the papal mass on July 28 as a giant sleepover party. The site was a former air force base turned national park in northwestern Toronto. To get there, hundreds of thousands of people lugged sleeping bags, backpacks and a tapestry of flags on a ten-kilometre pilgrimage through the streets of the city. Finally, they marched past a cache of military trucks, tanks and guns in search of a spot to camp near an ornate stage adorned with a towering 50-metre cross. Five field hospitals and 12 first-aid units were on standby to handle any emergencies. Dehydration and heat exhaustion were the main concerns, and organizers had 2.6 million bottles of water to hand out. "It's like one big sleepover party with hundreds of thousands of your Christian brothers and sisters," said Danielle Sweet, 13, whose pilgrimage began in her hometown of Adelborough, Massachusetts.

The image quickly changed from sleepover to refugee camp as Saturday's fierce sun vanished behind a veil of cloud. Pilgrims grabbed cardboard boxes and

◀ Wade Kohoko of Algonquin First Nation in Ontario waits for the arrival of the Pope at the vigil ceremony at Downsview Park. (Kevin Frayer/CP)

Pilgrims listen to Pope John Paul speak at the Saturday vigil. (Left to right: Robert Bukaty/AP; Kevin Frayer/CP)

chunks of plastic guardrail to help build makeshift tents. But the rain held off as the Pope arrived by helicopter and made his way through the massive crowd in his popemobile. He touched off a scramble of adulation as many pilgrims ran frantically to keep up with him. "I'm so excited, I feel sick," said Gina Emanual, 16, of Rochester, New York, as the popemobile drove by. A swell of pilgrims, some knocking others to the ground, others trampling lawn chairs and tents in the excitement, followed in its wake.

Once on the stage, the Pope was wheeled out atop a platform. He waved to the crowd amid chants of "John Paul II, we love you." Eventually, the crowd fell silent as he greeted them with a reminder that they represent the future of the Roman Catholic Church and thanked them for their enthusiasm and spirit. "In you, gathered from the four corners of the world, the church sees her future," he said in a strong but muffled voice.

Pope John Paul II | 101

The World Youth Day cross towers over pilgrims at the Sunday mass at Downsview Park. (Kevin Frayer/CP)

Pilgrims listen to Pope John Paul speak at the Saturday vigil. (Kevin Frayer/CP)

The World Youth Day participants, their faces lit by candlelight, listened raptly as the pontiff encouraged them "to build, brick by brick, the city of God within the city of man." John Paul's words seemed to leave his young devotees inspired and invigorated. "We are the future, and that means it's our responsibility to tell the other kids there's more to life than bars and drinking," said Stephano Glasweta, 18, of London, England. "I think he's given me the courage to do that when I go home." The Pope also blessed hundreds of pilgrims who streamed up and down a massive staircase leading to the stage before he left to return to his lodgings at Morrow Park, a retirement home for nuns in Toronto.

A pilgrim holds up a candle at the Downsview Park vigil. (Tom Hanson/CP)

"You are the men and women of tomorrow. The future is in your hearts and in your hands. God is entrusting to you the task, at once difficult and uplifting, of working with Him in the building of the civilization of love."

–Pope John Paul II, July 27, 2002

Pilgrims welcome the Pope as he arrives on stage for the vigil. (Kevin Frayer/CP)

The pilgrims, meanwhile, camped out to await his return the next day for mass. Some spent the hours celebrating or trading pins and flags with new friends from foreign countries. "There were parties going on all around us all night," said Brittney Henderson, 15, of Brampton, Ontario. "These French Polynesian guys were teaching us their traditional dances and the Polish people had a parade."

Then, just after dawn, the rain came, turning Downsview Park into a mucky bog. Garbage bags, pup tents and tarpaulins provided little protection from the gusts of wind that whipped umbrellas inside out. The rain drove some pilgrims home but most, anxious to glimpse the Pope once more, were undaunted. "Even if it had started snowing, I would have stayed. It's the Pope," said Tom Stachowski, 18, of Dearborn, Michigan. Others took a more spiritual view of the stormy conditions. "I think it was God's wake-up call because we didn't have alarm clocks," said Paulo Coquim, 34, of Brantford, Ontario.

◀ Pilgrims pray with the Pope at the Saturday vigil.
(Gabriel Bouys/Pool/CP)

Against a backdrop screen of trees, the Pope speaks from the stage
of the World Youth Day papal mass. (Kevin Frayer/CP)

The mass

▲ World flags adorn the stage at the papal mass. (Kevin Frayer/CP)

A Hollywood screenwriter couldn't have come up with a better script. The day that Pope John Paul was to lead a mass for 800,000 people gathered at Downsview Park started with a torrential downpour of biblical proportions. Then the sun broke through the clouds – if only momentarily – as he spoke. For some Roman Catholics who had waited through a soggy night to see their spiritual leader, the experience defied description. "This is what it's all about. I don't know how to put it into words," said Alexander Ward, 27, of Marietta, Ohio, as he surveyed the sea of people stretched out for a kilometre in front of the giant stage.

The strains of Handel's Hallelujah Chorus echoed through the driving rain as Pope John Paul arrived to greet the soaked, sprawling congregation. The pontiff's helicopter throbbed into view shortly before 9 a.m. before vanishing behind an ornate outdoor stage. "The Pope is here, the Pope is here," exclaimed Gloria Rodriguez of Toronto. "My hair is absolutely standing on end. I can't believe the Pope has actually come here to bless us." Minutes later, thunderous cheers rang out

"You are young and the Pope is old and a bit tired. But he still fully identifies with your hopes and aspirations. Although I have lived through much darkness, under harsh totalitarian regimes, I have seen enough evidence to be unshakably convinced that no difficulty, no fear is so great that it can completely suffocate the hope that springs eternal in the hearts of the young.

▲ Pilgrims celebrate during the Pope's arrival ceremony. (Robert Bukaty/AP)

▲ One young pilgrim reacts to John Paul's arrival at the papal welcoming ceremony. (Kevin Frayer/CP)

"Do not let that hope die! Stake your lives on it! We are not the sum of our weaknesses and failures; we are the sum of the Father's love for us and our real capacity to become the image of his son . . . .

"My wish for all of you who are here is that the commitments you have made during these days of faith and celebration will bring forth abundant fruits of dedication and witness. May you always treasure the memory of Toronto!"

Pope John Paul II, July 28, 2002

as the Pope reappeared in the popemobile, its windows open as he waved to the crowd.

The ranks of the devoted had been swelling through the early morning hours as Catholics and the curious alike arrived to witness the public service and lay eyes on John Paul in person. For some, the wind and pelting rain was too much; they were streaming toward the exits even as the Pope spoke. But many seemed not to notice the weather, standing rapt as hymns rang clearly through the muggy air. They listened solemnly as John Paul, in his homily, introduced one of the toughest issues facing the Catholic Church: a string of sex abuse scandals involving clergy, mainly in the United States and Europe. "The harm done by some priests and religious to the young and vulnerable fills us all with a deep sense of sadness and shame," he told the crowd. "But think of the vast majority of dedicated and generous priests whose only wish is to serve and do good . . . be close to them and support them." His remarks prompted a chorus of cheers and applause, some from among the hundreds of priests gathered on stage to deliver communion. Not everyone was pleased – some advocates for the victims of sexually abusive priests complained later that the Pope seemed to sympathize more with priests than with those who were molested.

Overall, however, the World Youth Day crowd did not come from around the world to criticize the Pope, but to celebrate their faith with him. Participants said the experience of travelling to another country for the event changed the way they viewed their faith. "It makes you look at it a whole lot differently from when you're at home," said Jessie Jerkovich, 15, from Hackensack, Minnesota. "It makes you realize it's everyone. You're not alone, it's the whole entire world."

▲ Bishops try to stay dry while they wait for the papal mass to begin.
(Kevin Frayer/CP)

◄ Priests stand during a prayer by John Paul during the mass.
(Kevin Frayer/CP)

Pope John Paul II | 111

The farewell

John Paul boards his plane at Pearson Airport in Toronto.
(Kevin Frayer/CP)

Cheers, tears and soaring choral music mingled with the roar of jet engines as Pope John Paul's visit to Canada ended on July 29, 2002, with one last display of the vitality and spirit he showed during the six days he spent in the Toronto area, surrounded by the world's Catholic youth. About 50 delighted World Youth Day pilgrims who had gathered at a Toronto airport hangar broke into the familiar chant of "John Paul II, we love you" as the pontiff hoisted his bent, elderly frame up a steep staircase, supported by a handrail on one side and an aide on the other. Upon reaching the top,

▲ John Paul waves a final goodbye. (Kevin Frayer/CP)

the Pope gave a final wave to the adoring crowd of dignitaries, politicians and Youth Day participants before disappearing inside the jet, which was headed to Guatemala.

Veteran Vatican observers had been surprised by the Pope, who finished every one of his public engagements in Toronto despite obvious physical frailties. "He taught us, I think, that despite physical infirmity and suffering and age and pain, one can still have great value and be golden," said Father Tom Rosica, national director of World Youth Day. Tears streamed

Pilgrims wave flags from their home countries as they listen to the Pope during a welcoming ceremony. (Paul Chiasson/CP)

down Esperanza Martinez's cheeks as she mouthed a silent prayer and held her hands to the sky, a blue rosary dangling from her forearm, as the Pope's plane taxied away. "I'm here because I feel like he needs our blessing; he needs our prayers. He gives so much, I wanted to give him back a little bit." Even non-Catholics who were on hand for the Pope's departure were moved to tears by the sight of him. "We have

> "We have seen God in pictures, but this is a living god, who can bring the whole world together under one roof."
>
> —Amarjeet Sidhu, July 29, 2002

seen god in pictures, but this is a living God, who can bring the whole world together under one roof," sobbed Amarjeet Sidhu, a Sikh whose daughter attended a Catholic school in Toronto. "There are so many things going on in the world. People like this are very rare and it's only once in a while in your life you can see them."

Acknowledgements

▲ Pope John Paul II gives his Easter Sunday blessing from his studio's window at the Vatican on March 27, 2005. (Osservatore Romano/AP)

The stories and photographs in this book have been taken from the files of The Canadian Press and its writers and photographers who followed Pope John Paul II almost non-stop during his three visits to Canada. On a major story like a papal visit, field reporters often feed material to a central desk that edits and shapes the story, so bylines, if assigned at all, may not reflect the work of all who contributed to the coverage. It is therefore impossible to give credit to everyone whose work contributed to this book. The editors' thanks go to all of those CP journalists, current and past, not just to the ones listed below, whose hard work helped make Pope John Paul II: Connecting to Canadians possible.

The Canadian Press (CP) is Canada's national news agency. Since 1917, CP's teams of reporters, photographers and broadcasters have reported on the Canadian story, sharing our experiences coast to coast and around the world. With bureaus and seasoned, award-winning editorial staff across the country, The Canadian Press covers everything from politics to pop culture, company news to sports results, in French and English.

Writers:
Nicole Baer, Andrea Baillie, Larry Black, Irwin Block, Jim Coyle, Judy Cross, Linda Drouin, Steve Fairbairn, Andrew Flynn, Paul Gessell, Barbara Gunn, Jen Horsey, Walter Krevenchuk, Kathryn Leger, Mark Lisac, Gary Mason, Wendy McCann, James McCarten, Elaine McCluskey, Penny MacRae, Tom McDougall, Robert MacPherson, Ken MacQueen, Felicity Munn, Nelle Oosterom, Angela Pacienza, Gary Regenstreif, Glenn Somerville, Sylvia Strojek, Allan Swift, John Ward.

Photographers:
Doug Ball, Peter Bregg, Dave Buston, Fred Chartrand, Paul Chiasson, Hans Deryk, Kevin Frayer, Frank Gunn, Tom Hanson, Aaron Harris, Ryan Remiorz, Chuck Stoody.